D0993320

theatre & voice

Theatre &
Series Editors: Jen Harvie and Dan Rebellato

Published
Joel Anderson: *Theatre & Photography*
Susan Bennett: *Theatre & Museums*
Bill Blake: *Theatre & the Digital*
Colette Conroy: *Theatre & the Body*
Emma Cox: *Theatre & Migration*
Jim Davis: *Theatre & Entertainment*
Jill Dolan: *Theatre & Sexuality*
Helen Freshwater: *Theatre & Audience*
Jen Harvie: *Theatre & the City*
Nadine Holdsworth: *Theatre & Nation*
Erin Hurley: *Theatre & Feeling*
Dominic Johnson: *Theatre & the Visual*
Joe Kelleher: *Theatre & Politics*
Ric Knowles: *Theatre & Interculturalism*
Petra Kuppers: *Theatre & Disability*
Patrick Lonergan: *Theatre & Social Media*
Caoimhe McAvinchey: *Theatre & Prison*
Bruce McConachie: *Theatre & Mind*
Lucy Nevitt: *Theatre & Violence*
Helen Nicholson: *Theatre & Education*
Lourdes Orozco: *Theatre & Animals*
Lionel Pilkington: *Theatre & Ireland*
Benjamin Poore: *Theatre & Empire*
Paul Rae: *Theatre & Human Rights*
Alan Read: *Theatre & Law*
Dan Rebellato: *Theatre & Globalization*
Trish Reid: *Theatre & Scotland*
Nicholas Ridout: *Theatre & Ethics*
Jo Robinson: *Theatre & the Rural*
Juliet Rufford: *Theatre & Architecture*
Rebecca Schneider: *Theatre & History*
Lara Shalson: *Theatre & Protest*
Kim Solga: *Theatre & Feminism*
Konstantinos Thomaidis: *Theatre & Voice*
Fintan Walsh: *Theatre & Therapy*
Eric Weitz: *Theatre & Laughter*
David Wiles: *Theatre & Time*
Harvey Young: *Theatre & Race*

Forthcoming
Matt Delbridge: *Theatre & Technology*
Kate Elswit: *Theatre & Dance*
Paul Murphy: *Theatre & Class*
Keren Zaiontz: *Theatre & Festivals*

theatre &
voice

Konstantinos Thomaidis

 macmillan education palgrave

First published 2017 by
PALGRAVE

Palgrave in the UK is an imprint of Macmillan Publishers Limited,
registered in England, company number 785998, of 4 Crinan Street,
London, N1 9XW.

Palgrave® and Macmillan® are registered trademarks in the United States,
the United Kingdom, Europe and other countries.

ISBN 978–1–137–55249–5 paperback

This book is printed on paper suitable for recycling and made from fully
managed and sustained forest sources. Logging, pulping and manufacturing
processes are expected to conform to the environmental regulations of the
country of origin.

A catalogue record for this book is available from the British Library.

A catalog record for this book is available from the Library of Congress.

Printed in China

For Natalia

contents

Series editors' preface   ix

Foreword by Norie Neumark   xi

Following a voice   1

   Rethinking voice in performance   8

Voicing speech   13

   Voice as sonorous material or voice as
language and ideas?   23

Voicing music   30

   More than sound?   35

Bodies voicing   45

   Training voices: embodying more than technique?   50

Voices beyond bodies   57

   Many voices and voices of the many   65

Conclusion: from voice to voicing 71

Further Reading 75
Bibliography 77
Index 84
Acknowledgements 89

series editors' preface

The theatre is everywhere, from entertainment districts to the fringes, from the rituals of government to the ceremony of the courtroom, from the spectacle of the sporting arena to the theatres of war. Across these many forms stretches a theatrical continuum through which cultures both assert and question themselves. Theatre has been around for thousands of years, and the ways we study it have changed decisively. It's no longer enough to limit our attention to the canon of Western dramatic literature. Theatre has taken its place within a broad spectrum of performance, connecting it with the wider forces of ritual and revolt that thread through so many spheres of human culture. In turn, this has helped make connections across disciplines; over the past 50 years, theatre and performance have been deployed as key metaphors and practices with which to rethink gender, economics, war, language, the fine arts, culture and one's sense of self.

Theatre & is a long series of short books which hopes to capture the restless interdisciplinary energy of theatre and performance. Each book explores connections between theatre and some aspect of the wider world, asking how the theatre might illuminate the world and how the world might illuminate the theatre. Each book is written by a leading theatre scholar and represents the cutting edge of critical thinking in the discipline.

We have been mindful, however, that the philosophical and theoretical complexity of much contemporary academic writing can act as a barrier to a wider readership. A key aim for these books is that they should all be readable in one sitting by anyone with a curiosity about the subject. The books are challenging, pugnacious, visionary sometimes and, above all, clear. We hope you enjoy them.

Jen Harvie and Dan Rebellato

foreword

and & and // & *and* &

& entangled

Theatre & voice – all the more entangled here with an amper-sand ... an ampersand that is the very evocation of entan-glement. Like voice, with voice, an ampersand speaks of entanglement.

& hinged

Hinging voice & theatre, the ampersand proposes that the two co-compose each other. It's as if they always spoke to each other, most intimately. As if they belong together. And they do. & they do.

And voice

Voice, after all, is comfortable with intimate speaking and performing – and with invoking intimate social relations. As it breathes from one body to another, connecting them, tincturing the atmosphere between them, contouring the spaces they share, voice begins with the intimate and moves out – in and out & out and in.

& voice

As it moves, voice tunes us in and attunes us ... sounding and connecting, composing & co-composing – bodies, spaces, texts, performances, theatres. And it unsettles as it reverberates. Theatre unsettled by voice – the certainties of both unfixed – this is what the book promises us, and this is what it enacts.

and & and // & and &

I sense I'm having a Gertrude Stein moment, provoked by the ampersand. No surprise, perhaps, since voice was certainly something Stein knew how to play with. And if, as she proposes, a *postdramatic* play is a 'landscape', and painters should use their ears (and writers their eyes), then sound and voice need to come to the fore in theatre. And in writing about theatre ... And they do in what follows.

Theatre and// *Theatre* & ... is what follows as 'disciplinary certainties' are left behind.

and & and. & and &

In what follows, you can listen to heterogeneous voices and apprehend anew the diversity of theatre. As the call of voice resounds, it is a call to theatre studies and theatre practices to come to the party with voice theories and practices. It invites theatre studies to come & party, better late than never. Come on along, voice will be performing 'its subversive and disruptive workings'. You won't be disappointed.

& party

But, it also asks, is theatre studies a latecomer to this & party? Or rather, has it perhaps not noticed that it is already entangled, enmeshed with voice thinking and practices – with the thinking of practice and the thinking that is practice? Come on along. At this party, all theatre is welcome – performance, participatory, cross-media, and the rest – come as you are and be provoked and provocative.

& entangled

And so what follows are wonderful provocations to rethink, to imagine and re-imagine thinking and practice. If you come from the theatre side of the ampersand, your listening habits will be unsettled. If you come from the voice side of the ampersand, your sense of performative potentials will be expanded. And if you respond to the call of what follows and hover on the ampersand itself, you will experience the surprising connections and entanglements that is theatre & voice.

Norie Neumark is a sound/media artist and theorist (www.out-of-sync.com). Her monograph Voicetracks: Attuning to Voice in Media and the Arts *(MIT Press, 2017) explores voice and the new materialist turn. Based in Melbourne, she is an Honorary Professorial Fellow at VCA and Emeritus Professor at La Trobe University, as well as being founding editor of* Unlikely: Journal for Creative Arts *(http://unlikely.net.au).*

theatre & voice

Following a voice

It is late morning on a cloudy Friday in July. We are a group of approximately fifty people standing amidst elaborate tombs and impressive mausoleums near the Gambetta entrance of Père Lachaise Cemetery in Paris. We stand in silence, or those of us who arrived in pairs or small groups keep our voices low and sporadically exchange a few whispered utterances. We have all been given a headset attached to a portable receiver through which we listen to ambient music and the periodic instruction not to wander too far away. The volume of the music fades out and it is this moment of palpable tension between dying music and impending silence which signals that we are about to transform from a gathering of strangers to an itinerant collective of participants. *Remote Paris*, a performative audio tour devised by Berlin-based company Rimini Protokoll, is about to begin.

1

'Welcome to the cemetery. We thank you for taking the path and for making it here,' announces a pre-recorded voice through the headphones. 'Look around you. The trees. The monuments. The tombs. Search for a tombstone that interests you.' We scatter around and, following the voice's instructions, embark on an unusual journey through the city. Stefan Kaegi's (1972–) project, under the general title *Remote X*, has been performed around the globe, always in direct dialogue with the site within which it unfolds. Not only pathways, but also instructions, scripted texts and voice recordings (always in the local language) are adapted to the new locale. In its 2015 iteration for Paris Quartier d'Été festival, we are invited to stroll through the Parisian cemetery reflecting on the lives of our chosen deceased and the inevitable passing of time. We observe passers-by and listen out to the sounds of the city as we exit the eerily quiet opening 'setting' of the piece. We take the underground and dance – some of us more excitedly than others – to Van Halen's 1983 hit song 'Jump'. We march and stage an impromptu protest. We treat ourselves to a sing-along version of Louise Attaque's 'J't'emmène au vent', the 1997 folk-rock track from the debut album of the French band sung by Gaëtan Roussel. We lie on the grass and listen to imaginary raindrops, reflecting on our distance from the clouds above. We ponder further the limits of our ephemeral bodies by looking around the entrance of Hôpital Saint-Louis in the 10th arrondissement, prompted to guess who is a patient and why they are here. We compete with each other in jogging and we cheer basketball players exercising in an open-air court between multi-storey, concrete buildings. For the end of the piece, the voice takes us to the top of the iconic Headquarters of the French Communist Party, designed by Oscar Niemeyer, and lets us look over the city, tracing our trajectory from above while a smoke machine envelops us in 'the clouds'.

The project poses vital questions around how bodies occupy and inhabit public spaces, the limits and capabilities of the very condition of having a physical body, and the types of encounter between individual subject-bodies that can render them into the body politic. It is, however, the role of voice in the piece that seems the most complex, provocative and intriguing to unpack. Habitual discussions of theatre and voice may presume a rehearsed or devised playtext, vocal choices such as accent, resonance and inflection made by appropriately trained actors, and the shared presence of speakers and listeners within an acoustically viable theatre space. Playful nods to such presuppositions can still be traced in this instance, yet, in many ways, *Remote Paris* interrogates what voices 'normally' do in the theatre and calls for an examination of voice that is attuned to contemporary, participatory and cross-media practices. As I walk, dance or march along to the voiced instructions in my ears, I keep thinking of the phrase that Sarah Butcher, founding member of the British collective non zero one, used in a recent conversation to describe how the company employs headphone voices in its audio-based, installatory or promenade work: 'The voice is the guide to the experience as well as the experience itself' (in Thomaidis and Butcher, 2016, p. 76). How does voice shape or contribute to our experiences in *Remote Paris*? If voice is *the experience itself*, what are the characteristics of this experience and how do we begin to talk about it in meaningful ways?

Here, we first encounter voice as sound. It is an acoustic phenomenon, the transmission and auditory reception of resonant vibrations. Its intonation and colour are part of an enfolding composition that sets a particular tone and atmosphere, not unlike uses of voice more readily identifiable as music. But the recorded voice in this instance is not simply *presented* as sound. It also *does* something to our hearing; it *reorganizes* the aural field available to us by damping much of the noisy soundscape of the city. It also overpowers any other sounds intimated to us through the headphones. To use composer and acoustic ecologist R. Murray Schafer's term, this voice is a 'sound signal' (1977, p. 9), a foreground sound that sticks out from the constant background of music that forms the soundtrack of our listening experience. In other words, the way voice is recorded and performed redirects our attention in ways that imply that it is more important than other elements of the overall 'composition'. Voice also communicates written information, the instructions scripted by Kaegi and his team. In this sense, this voice can be thought of as spoken text, although this particular textual field seems surprisingly open: the voice reacts to our choices and is timed to intervene at moments of hesitation or too much autonomy and initiative on our part. As a foreigner relying only on the

Francophone utterances to be guided through an unfamiliar to me urban environment, I am all too aware of the linguistic parameters of such text-driven interaction (and fortuitously thankful that the six years of attending a French-Greek school as a teenager have not gone to waste). Knowing that the piece was first presented in Germany and then was recreated around the globe, I am also aware that some passages of the voiced text are recomposed and translated. The voice I hear is linguistically adapted and adaptable, and, in each occasion, presupposes a given linguistic community for its one-directional communication to be successful.

Significantly, voice is also functional. It is a literal 'guide to the experience', like a voiced map or a GPS operating detached from its visual counterparts. Voice structures space and locates us within places in playful and unexpected ways. It serves an 'anchor function', to borrow from Axel Stockburger's analysis of voice in multiplayer video and computer games: 'this anchoring provides a kind of bridge that crosses the potential feeling of spatial disjunction and enables situation of the subject in the simulated environment' (2010, pp. 296–297). In our case, the voice anchors us in the real-life environment in ways that help turn it into our 'playing field'; and, if we think of ourselves as audiences immersed in a performance experience, the voice serves to construct the urban space as the scenography of our *theatre*. The voice does not only tell us where to go and what to do. It also tells us who we are. From time to time, it addresses us as a 'horde' – *its* horde, as a matter of fact, for which it has a special kind of responsibility and over which it exerts special kinds of authority. In being addressed as the horde and in responding to such an appellation by complying with the instructions, we become the voice's horde. It is as if the voice makes us the listeners it wishes to have in order to generate particular effects. These effects have to do with performance (*co-creating, participating and paying attention to a structured experience or event*) but also with ideology. Listening to the voice individually and as a group materializes the unspoken assumption that the voice knows more than we do, that we need to accept its omnipresence and compelling potency over us, or that we could potentially develop a dialogue with it by having a certain input in the decisions made throughout the journey and in the ways we interact with each other as a collective.

Yet, if we are a 'horde', who is the voice? Is it a character, an imaginary persona with designated characteristics, partaking in the same performed world we are invited to inhabit for the duration of the piece? Is it a person, a non-theatrical individual initiating a direct contact with us through sounds and words? Is it a substitute, standing in for the author and deviser to direct our actions and transform them into a performance score? Let us hear what the voice has to say, soon after the performance begins, about itself – in fact, about *herself*:

> Can we be on first-name terms? Nice to meet you. My name is Margaux. My voice, is it familiar to you? Does it remind you of someone? Do you

imagine a face when you listen to me? What do my eyes look like? What do my lips look like when I speak? Lips are something that you can kiss. But I don't have lips. I don't have a mouth. Is my voice strange? I know. Everybody finds it strange. My voice sounds a bit artificial. Excuse me for that. This is because I'm not human. But I want to speak words nonetheless. Trust me and put your mobile phones on mute. For you, there isn't going to be any voice other than mine. (my translation)

We are made aware that this voice is artificial, synthesized, that is, through text-to-speech technology of the kind that has become familiar through automated phone banking, accessibility software, railway and airport announcements or mobile phone technology. This voice might have a name, but it is not annexed to a physical body. It knows it did not originate within the material contours of a human face or throat, but it happily draws attention to this lack. Its design might make it sound monotonously pleasant and alarmingly reassuring, but, as we are to find out while our journey progresses, it can also be personable, poetic, instructive, authoritarian, malleable, untrustworthy and uplifting. During *Remote Paris*, we listen to a voice that is at once sound and text, that fulfils both aesthetic and ideological functions, and that poses more questions about its identity, and identity in general, than it answers. It can be both a friendly companion and an assertive autocrat. Jokingly lighthearted or vexedly serious, for all we know, this voice is a problem.

Rethinking voice in performance

The aim of this short book is none other than to reintroduce voice *as a problem* to the field of theatre and performance studies. An introductory book on theatre *and* voice is faced with the impossibility of a myriad of options for content. From speaking poetic text to the professional techniques required for belting out musical theatre solos, and from the role of voice in theatre in community settings to voice-over acting and the amateur or everyday voices used as material for verbatim practices, voice and performance intersect in multiple and diverse ways. In fact, any adequate discussion of voice could only be imagined through a whole new *'Voice &'* series of short monographs. This text will touch on a few of the above areas, but its purpose will not be to provide a detailed overview. Rather, I aim to highlight and critique some of the assumptions we might have when we deal with voice as theatre-goers, scholars and practitioners and argue for the potential that theatre and performance afford in undercutting, subverting and re-imagining established expectations around voice. This re-examination is timely and highly necessary given the recent rise in academic interest around voice and the reluctant and overdue engagement of theatre studies with this revitalized interest in voice. Still, the goal here is not merely to offer original, thought-provoking discussion. New ways of thinking about voice can lead to fresh ways of practising voice in performance, and, vice versa, contemporary, emerging ways of performing with and through voice pressingly require new frameworks for understanding and conceptualizing it.

When attempting to do so, however, we are faced with a significant paucity of critical writing on voice within theatre studies. Texts such as J.L. Austin's *How to Do Things with Words* (1962), for example, were foundational in the type of thinking that paved the way for the consolidation of the research field we now understand as performance studies. Even though Austin's well-rehearsed argument is that utterances such as oaths or orders are performative acts in that they do not simply describe realities or make statements but can also produce tangible results, voice is not considered in any detail. In fact, many of Austin's examples rely on the practice of voicing these utterances and receiving them as listeners situated in given circumstances. Still, voice does not enter the discussion – and this is also the case with most of the foundational texts of performance studies. In his seminal *Performance Studies: An Introduction* ([2001] 2013), Richard Schechner did not draw on any voice-related examples, at least in any comprehensive or explicit way, and the same applies to Eugenio Barba and Nicola Savarese's project of developing *A Dictionary of Theatre Anthropology* ([1991] 2005). Skipping to Bryan Reynolds's more recent *Performance Studies: Key Words, Concepts and Theories* (2014), a robust showcase of the terminologies that performance studies has conceived and developed in its proliferative and expansive discourses, not much seems to have changed: only the entry on the notion of the 'interval' touches on aspects that could be related to voice.

Similarly scarce is the analytical writing on the intersections of theatre and voice in key scholarly periodicals of
broader interest to the theatre and performance commu-
nities; the special issues of *Performance Research* on 'Voices'
(MacDonald, 2003) and of *Studies in Musical Theatre* on
'Voice and Excess' (Taylor, 2012) are notable exceptions.
The American Association for Theatre in Higher Education
(ATHE) might have a 'Voice and Speech Trainers' focus group
(which, however, focuses mostly on the field of voice pedagogy), but the UK-based Theatre and Performance Research
Association (TaPRA) or the International Federation for
Theatre Research (IFTR) do not include any such working groups. I cannot help but notice that in a multi-volume
series such as '*Theatre &*', which celebrates current thinking
around theatre, broadly conceived, the addition of *Theatre &
Voice* comes eight years after the first few titles in the catalogue went to print (and we are yet to read *Theatre & Sound*
or *Theatre & Music*).

Such lacks are neither incidental nor accidental. To a
certain extent, they are programmatic. The trajectory from
drama, as an area of interest, to theatre studies, and then to
the broad spectrum of performance studies, was premised
on a polemic against conventional understandings of theatre
as bound to text. As a consequence, voice – conventionally
seen as speech – might have fallen victim to its close
association with spoken text and sung lyrics in theatre
practices. On the other hand, these gaps are the effect of
mono-disciplinarity, of operating within quite distinct fields
of practice and scholarly enquiry. When working with voice

within neatly defined disciplines, what voice can be and what voice can do might be taken for granted. Speech trainers, singing teachers, dialect coaches or sound designers and technicians always and already know what voice is within their respective fields. This strand of work is necessary in that it fosters technical development and expertise. What it might prohibit, however, is a reconsideration of common and core presuppositions about voice. Does voice always equal efficient or regionally convincing speaking? Are powerful projection and crispy articulation always necessary? Does good voicing equal technical singing or admirably athletic melodic feats? Is voice only a quantifiable, measurable, recordable and reproducible acoustic phenomenon? Do any of these questions have any relevance to the voice in *Remote Paris*? If not, how can we approach it? The proposed strategy here is that of interdisciplinarity. My discussion will draw on methodologies, terms and discourses from various fields, from philosophy, musicology, psychoanalysis and linguistics to cinema and opera studies, in order to facilitate a re-examination of voice in theatre. Correspondingly, 'theatre' will be taken as an umbrella term. The word on the left side of the book title's ampersand will represent a continuum of practices including text, devised and immersive theatre, opera, musical theatre, installations, performance and sound art, in the hope that leaving disciplinary certainties behind can unsettle habitual ways of listening to voice.

A second gap this book proposes to redress, or at least bring attention to, is the lack of sustained interactions between voice theory and writing on theatre. From Aristotle,

Quintilian and Augustine to Levinas, Adorno and Derrida, there is a significant corpus of philosophical works that proposes ways to understand voice as part of larger discussions on ethics, identity and politics. However, in the last quarter of the twentieth century and the first decade of the twenty-first in particular, thinkers in a variety of fields have taken to voice as the main focus of their texts. Such works include those by Carolyn Abbate, John Potter, Michel Chion, Steven Connor, Mladen Dolar and Adriana Cavarero, whom I retro-spectively perceive as a first generation of voice studies schol-ars. Some specialists on voice and sound may have entered into a dialogue with these propositions, but, for the most part, the theatre community has ignored these significant contributions. Even the occasional monograph that is refresh-ingly attuned to the theatrical voice seems to circumvent or condense any reference to this expanding body of work (Inchley, 2015, pp. 6, 12; Kimbrough, 2011, pp. 6–8, 205). If this seems a minor omission, one has only to compare it to the expansive vocabularies around the body – derived from dance, somatics, affect theory, cognitive materialism, race and gender studies – that permeate current theatre debates to fully comprehend the correspondent dearth in the critical examination of voice in the theatre. In the last decade, voice studies has emerged as an inter-discipline and this book is one of the first to systematically draw on the terminologies and concerns of this new field in order to bring them to bear on theatre and performance studies. Key terms and ideas will be introduced, applied and critiqued in the following sections, alongside a broad range of case studies. The main purpose is to advance an argument in favour of practising and thinking through voice less as a certainty or commonplace 'object' and more in its subversive and disruptive workings. Having said that, this approach is equally informed by the hope that a more rounded understanding of voice can significantly enhance the pleasure we can take in performing, thinking about and listening to voices in theatrical contexts.

Voicing speech

To explore voices in their most quotidian manifestation on the theatrical stage, it is worth considering the relation between voice and text – or, to put it more emphatically, voice as speech. Much of the literature on theatre and voice, for example, consists of books authored by prominent speech trainers and mainly addressed to working professionals, with the aim of preparing them to tackle the demands of poetic text or more contemporary plays. The type of thinking that sees voice in performance as primarily bound to some form of text – from elaborate metric writing and translations to documentary sources and devised material – is so pervasive that it might at first appear that voicing and speaking are synonymous in the case of performance.

To begin to disentangle the vocal from the textual, I propose doing so 'from the inside' – by looking at a well-known text and a fairly recent, also notable and celebrated, production of this text: Deborah Warner's (1959–) staging of Sophocles's *Electra* (RSC/Barbican, UK, 1988; international tour, 1991–1992). The tragedy, performed for the first time as part of the festival of Dionysus in Athens near the end of the fifth century BCE, follows Electra's quest for revenge. Her father, Agamemnon, upon returning victorious from the Trojan War, was murdered by his wife Clytemnestra, who also seized the throne and now governs with her lover Aegisthus. Electra sent away her younger brother Orestes with his Pedagogue and spent years mourning her father's loss and yearning for Orestes's return. Years later, the first part of the play witnesses Electra mourning at the gates of the palace, and quarrelling with her mother and sister, Chrysothemis, who is more obedient towards the new rulers. In the second half, the Pedagogue falsely announces Orestes's death and, when Clytemnestra is relieved from the fear of her son's revenge, Orestes appears, is recognized by Electra, and kills his mother, while Electra celebrates. The play finishes with the siblings driving Aegisthus inside to complete their avengement. While the advancement of the plot and its resolution are rapid in the final episodes, for the most part, the play is static and reverberates with Electra's incessant mourning.

Fiona Shaw (1958–), embodying the title role in Warner's minimalist production, did not present an Electra that merely emits text, dialoguing, disagreeing or conspiring with other characters. Shaw found in Electra a woman 'who had been grieving every day for 12 years, wailing every day for 12 years [... and for whom she] had to sustain an emotional pitch almost to the breaking point' (de Vries, 1989). Mentions of Shaw's vocal work prevail in reviews. For example, Ian Shuttleworth acknowledged that this feverous voicing is part of the character's design but is also pursued to its limits by the performer: 'Hers is a character written on one note, but Shaw's one note (varying in volume, steady in sheer force) can cleave boulders' (1991). Two decades down the line, Greek theatre specialist Eleni Papazoglou dedicated most of her introduction to the Greek translation of Shaw's text 'Electra Speechless' to the actress's voice: 'thanks to a ferocious, unparalleled technique, her voice scratched – almost unbearably – the spectators' ears, constantly grabbed by the tightened rope of an inarticulate cry' (2011, p. 62, my translation). Warner and Shaw in a way extended the vocal interpretation that French director Antoine Vitez (1930–1990) had explored with actress Évelyne Istria in his three renditions of *Electra* (1966, 1971, 1986), as a vocality strained between the political arena of public discourse (succession to the throne, law, religion, rebellion) and personal psychology (grief, sexual frustration, family ties). Even earlier, Greek poet Yannis Ritsos (1909–1990), whose work was interpolated in the second *Electra* by Vitez, had the title character in his monologue *Orestes* (1962–1966) ponder about Electra's unforgiving voice: 'Listen to her – her voice spreads over her like a deep-arched vault,/and she herself is suspended in her voice/like the clapper of a bell, and is struck by and strikes the bell' (1993, p. 66). Electra's voice, from the extant text, through poetic re-workings, to contemporary productions, has been heard as decisive, unsettling and unsettled.

Why is Electra's voice so problematic? To sketch out a first response, I would like to consider another question first: what was the place of voice within tragedy and in the context of the Athenian nation-state more broadly? Aristotle (384–322 BCE) can offer some useful clues. Although writing several decades later, he draws on his direct experience of both the theatrical genre of tragedy and the political configuration of the Athenian democracy as they had been crystallized by the fourth century BCE. In his treatise on *Poetics* ([c.335 BCE] 1995), Aristotle proposed that the key components of tragic performance are six: *mythos* (story, plot or fable), *ethos* (character), *dianoia* (idea, thought), *opsis* (the visual aspects of performance), *lexis* (diction) and *melos* (song, musical melody). Theatre is conceived here as a multi-medium, hinging on the collaboration of various elements, and voice has a particular part to play in the overall synthesis. *Mythos*, *dianoia* and *ethos* are hierarchically more significant, while *lexis*, *opsis* and *melos* are only mediators of the plot, the ideas and the characters. *Lexis*, which is the element most closely linked with vocality in Aristotle's writing, derives from the same root as the verb *lego*, meaning either 'to speak' or 'to arrange/place in a particular order'. 'Diction' is not therefore an exact translation for *lexis*, which could be understood as a 'way of speaking' and/or a 'way of arranging (textual elements) in a particular order', most frequently associated in the actor's work with 'diction'. Aristotle assigns responsibility for this ordering to the actors; they need to be able to discern whether this arrangement designates 'a command, prayer, narrative, threat, question, [or] reply' (1995, p. 97), and speak it out appropriately.

In this scheme, words have a correct meaning and actors need to use their voices to communicate it. Their voices are rendered functional and, to a certain extent, predetermined by the supposedly fixed meaning embedded in the text. If we were to retrospectively apply here a model borrowed from media studies, the point could be summarized as follows: there is an *idea/message* proposed by the author, and the actor's job is to effect its *transmission* to the audience in such a way that the *means of this communication*, the voice, becomes transparent. Voices should not interfere (or propose alternatives). A similar logic was pursued by founder of modern linguistics Ferdinand de Saussure (1857–1913). In his theory of linguistic communication, meaning relies on the 'arrangement' of words/signs, on their relations, which are arbitrary and differential: the word 'table' has been arbitrarily chosen to communicate the idea 'table' for the English-speaking community, and it means 'table' only because it does not mean 'tree' or 'chair', for instance. Voice as sounding material is 'only a secondary thing, substance to be put to use' because the 'linguistic signifier … is not [in essence] phonic but incorporeal' (de Saussure, 1959, p. 118). The overarching scenario for both theorists is of striking similarity: an original, ideal meaning is rendered into corresponding spoken language, and the role of voice is to service this transition while effacing itself in the process. Ideas and language are to remain 'unstained' by voicing.

Electra's voice, however, resists idealized functionality and is not there to be forgotten. It moans, laments, screams, accuses and consistently offends. It throws a challenge to any ideal preconception of womanhood and of political correctness, exposes words as incapable of grasping her pain and need for vengeance, and renders language meaningless either by resorting to exclamations and non-verbal sounds or through sheer repetition. Her long monologues and dialogic exchanges 'say', time and again, the same thing, but language – even the shifting metres of poetic speech – is not enough to communicate it. It is a similar resistance to ideality that perhaps brought such palpable attention to Fiona Shaw's voice as Electra. In a panel discussion in 2001, a questioner criticized Shaw's performance for lacking 'magnificence and serenity' and hastened to provide further definitions: 'Magnificence is not screaming with a high pitched voice. It is low and resonant' (Poole, Warner & Shaw, 2002). It is not irrelevant to note that the speaker, who is of Greek origin, framed her remarks within the context of convention when addressing Shaw: 'you missed the magnificence of the ancient tradition that Greek performances seem to have' (Poole, Warner & Shaw, 2002). In this line of thinking, there is an ideal Electra, to be found in both the surviving text and the stock characterization of the title role in the canon of stagings, but Shaw's performance – qualified here as vocal performance and also described by the interlocutor as 'disturbing' – did not comply.

In *Poetics*, voice is not only reduced to an invisible bearer of linguistic meaning in the act of performance; it is also systematized as such in the analysis of the component parts of *lexis.* Aristotle presents a linear progression from letters and syllables to words and clauses, a progression on which modern phonology drew many of its methodologies to describe the synthesis of individual phonemes (elemental units of speech or sound) into larger clusters of spoken language. In Aristotle's understanding a letter is *phone adiairetos,* voice that cannot be divided further, and a syllable *phone asemos,* voice that does not have meaning, while clauses/utterances are termed *logos* and are *phone synthete semantike,* composite voice that has meaning. Voice starts as elemental sound but somewhere along the continuum becomes *logos,* speech, language, meaning.

This taxonomy resonates with Aristotle's thinking on the formation of nation-states, his treatise on *Politics.* An oft-cited passage distinguishes again between *voice* and *speech*:

> Man alone of the animals possesses speech. The mere voice, it is true, can indicate pain and pleasure, and therefore is possessed by the other animals as well [...], but speech is designed to indicate the advantageous and the harmful, and therefore also the right and the wrong; for it is the special property of man in distinction from the other animals that he alone has perception of good and bad and right and wrong and the other moral qualities, and it is partnership in these things that makes a household and a city-state. (Aristotle, [1932] 2014, p. 11)

Aristotle proposed not only that vocal elements are composed in the superior form of meaningful language, but also that this very ability is fundamental in facilitating the human species' move away from animal-like life and towards communal organization and citizenship.

In both cases, voice is only the first step for subsequent developments: from nonsensical phonemes to signifying utterances, and from animality to polity. In such analyses, voice is afforded a teleology; in other words, it is retrospectively seen as a prior and inferior state in an almost Darwinian evolution from animal to human, from emotion to thought, and from meaningless sound to meaningful language. Voice, if trained – as both professional 'tool' and means of sociability – and tamed accordingly, is to be turned into intelligible speech and to serve clarity of meaning. But how are these ideas played out in *Electra* and to what extent are they embodied in Electra's voice? The play presents a complex landscape of vocality. In the Prologue, for example, Orestes praises the Old Man/Pedagogue as a good listener and asks him to lend an attentive ear to his plans, which involve the false narrative of his death. His plans for revenge – a heavily political act given that he is the heir to the throne – require thoughtful discussion and the construction of convincing, albeit deceitful, speech. In the Second Episode, Clytemnestra prays to Apollo and concludes her speech by asking the god to attend even to what she keeps silent. It is as if this act of vertical listening requires a direct (and possible) communication between the unspoken voice and the ideality represented by the divine.

Electra, however, does not partake in the reasoning encapsulated in political discourse or the abstraction of silent interlocution. Her voice is un-tamed, and, although publicly heard, moves between screaming, cursing and a monotonous, escalating mourning. In fact, the entire performance of the play could be experienced as a constant attempt to regulate this voice and direct it towards speech (as effective linguistic exchange) or silence (as unuttered speech). The Chorus asks Electra to stop shouting at the doors of the palace, and Chrysothemis, her sister, finds her relentless weeping and wailing irrational. Clytemnestra inveighs against her daughter's unrestricted display of grief and silences her in order to pray. Even right after the recognition scene, Orestes and the Old Man also endeavour to keep her celebratory outbursts under control. The issue at stake is not that this voice is expressive of a particular emotion (grief, for the most part, or exultation, in the end). It is the sheer materiality of this vocal overflow – which exceeds regularized language and acts as a consistent reminder of the pre-political sounds of animalness – that all other characters fail to subdue. One could hear, then, in the dramaturgy of *Electra*, Aristotle's 'ascension' from voice to language not as a complete and finalized undertaking but as a struggle, as a project still in the making. Voice-*phone* still resists language-*logos*.

This monitoring of the vocal as a negotiation of the political is not limited to the exchange between characters and actors, but, crucially, involves the audience. I will detail such types of engagement in the following sections, but it is worth returning to Warner's *Electra* here as a preamble to this discussion.

As part of its international tour in 1991–1992, the production visited the Northern Irish city of Derry, which was at the epicentre of 'the Troubles' between Irish unionists and nationalists for years and had in fact witnessed more bloodshed in the week leading up to the performance. According to Shaw's recollections, audiences did not applaud after the performance and were 'unable to leave their seats, the power punch of Shaw's performance and the raw emotion still pulsating through the air after the cast had left the stage' (Muir, 2012). The actors returned on stage and engaged in a discussion with the audience, whose reactions ranged from condemning Electra's lingering on pain to directly accusing Shaw that she did not have the right to portray such pain because she had not lost anyone close to her (in fact, the actress's brother had recently been killed in an accident; see also Shaw, 1996). Aristotle might be useful in thinking through such responses. The local community was in the process of coming to terms with yet another collective trauma and this enterprise necessitated either silence or discussion – a regulation of voice – after the fervent vocal profusion that resounded between stage and auditorium. Nonetheless, Shaw's vocality, heard in this context, exceeded language even further. This Electra was not only a tirelessly mourning character embodied by an actress who opted for an unnerving pitch and dynamics of voicing; she was also an actress from the Republic of Ireland, sounding in her Southern Irish accent. Beyond vocal semiotics (language, speech and text), her phenomenal (real-life, present) voice must have added to the excess; this Electra sounded *too* close to home.

Voice as sonorous material or voice as language and ideas?

Such responsiveness to the materiality of voice poses vexed questions around the Aristotelian scheme of voice as self-effaced carrier of spoken ideas and as subjugated to political discourse. Aristotle was not alone in conceptualizing voice in such a disciplinatory and controlling fashion (and, in fact, his empirical interest in how speech is delivered by actors in *Poetics* leaves some space for elaboration on voice as experienced). Italian feminist theorist Adriana Cavarero (1947–) has recently shown how Western thinking, from Plato to poststructuralism, developed a bias against voice, placing it as hierarchically inferior to ideas and language, a tendency which she associated with logocentrism (2005, pp. 53–61). Cavarero counter-proposed a vocal philosophy of uniqueness that places the emphasis on voice as material, sonorous interchange between unique individualities: 'the voice manifests the *unique being* of each human being, and his or her spontaneous self-communication according to the rhythms of a sonorous relation' (2005, p. 173, original emphasis).

To a degree, her analysis is a riposte to French deconstructionist philosopher Jacques Derrida (1930–2004). His widely influential works, particularly *Of Grammatology* (1967) and *Voice and Phenomenon* (1967), took issue with what he saw as the privileging of voice over writing in Western philosophical discourse. He observed that a long tradition of philosophers has operated under the assumption that speech expresses our ideas and that writing is a secondary, subsidiary system, which is only useful to document or preserve speech.

However, Derrida's broader philosophical project was to propose that there is no completely uncontestable presence and that what is present is always 'contaminated' by its absent counterpart. In the case of speech and writing, it is not only that written text bears the trace of spoken text because it documents it. Inversely, speech always and already is marked by writing because when we speak, we mobilize signs (words, concepts, linguistic structures) that already pre-exist us. By virtue of putting to use a pre-existing language (or the pre-existing *premises* of a language that allow us to invent new words) or a set of pre-existing concepts when we speak, even what appears as a form of immediate communication, speech, is marked by the trace of antecedent writing, 'archi-writing' (Derrida, [1967] 2011, p. 73). Derrida found the only possibility for pure presence in the act of hearing oneself speak, when one is simultaneously the speaker and the listener of one's internal voice, without any recourse to any other auditor that may misinterpret one's ideas as expressed in words. Derrida's intention was not necessarily to counter-privilege writing over speech but to expose their co-dependence as a pairing of opposites. His thinking is useful in provoking more complex accounts of the act of speaking in the theatre, for example: is an actor's spoken delivery straightforwardly and unproblematically present because it takes place in the moment of addressing an audience? Isn't this 'presence' tainted by the 'absent' writing (play, improvised text or codes and styles of acting), the past of previous performances and the expectation of future performances? However, it is important to stress that

Derrida's preoccupation with voice is primarily concerned with speech (spoken language) and the ideal voice of internal interlocution that takes place 'without the aid of any exteriority' (Derrida, [1967] 2011, p. 69). For Cavarero, the voice of ideality and the voice of speech are still *logos*, as they are tied to ideas and language. Voices, however, can do much more than speak texts or allude to ideas, and another way to account for the complexity of presence is not by turning back to the interiority of the self but by opening out to the intersubjective communication between material bodies.

To mark the difference in approach, I propose a brief diversion towards a contemporary operatic performance. American soprano Juliana Snapper, in collaboration with composer Andrew Infanti, devised and performed the *Five Fathoms Opera Project* (MoMA PS1, NYC, 2008, and international tour). The site-specific underwater opera was performed in pools or water tanks, and was intended as a reflection on ecological disaster and adaptability. Snapper sang close to the water, intermittently continuing under its surface against a backdrop of electronic sound and with the participation of a local choir. From a Cavarerian perspective, in this instance, language, clarity of sung text and conventional operatic singing were dissolved and the audience was left to experience the directedness of Snapper's sonority. As voice studies scholar Nina Eidsheim has pointed out, 'Snapper reminds us that *what* we hear depends as much on our materiality, physicality, cultural and social histories, as it does on so-called objective measurements (decibel level, soundwave count, or score)' and helps us consider 'music as a material endeavour' (2015, p. 116, original emphasis). Derridean analysis would counter that Snapper's vocalization, although potentially perceived as mere sound, relies on the very existence of the operatic songs that were gradually deconstructed underwater as well as on audiences' expectations and prior knowledge of opera to gain its particular dynamic. The point, perhaps, is not to resolve these contradictions, but to draw attention to the fact that – much like Electra's 'unresolved' voice – this playing out of the tension between voice, language and writing acquires considerable potential in performance.

Twentieth- and twenty-first-century musicians have methodically explored the potential of such tensions. This is particularly the case with composers and sing-ers with a keen interest in interdisciplinary crossovers between areas traditionally demarcated as theatre or music. Armenian-American composer-singer Cathy Berberian (1925–1983), for instance, wrote and performed the solo *Stripsody* (1966) in order to question predominant views of song as music bound to text. Her inspiration from comic strip noises and her graphic score – which was not based on the precise alignment of lyrics to notes found in Western clas-sical compositions but on suggestive imagery – challenged 'the listeners' preconceptions of the ontology of the oper-atic voice as always and already "scored"' (Verstraete, 2014, p. 68). Berberian's work was not only pioneering in confronting the logocentric privileging of the composer/ author over (sung) text and of (sung) text over voice; it was also revelatory in foregrounding the pleasure, enjoyment and humorous exuberance that can be derived from such an undertaking. The deliberate pursuit to unfasten and release voice from language has informed a series of multidisciplinary works, including Phil Minton's (1940–) *Feral Choir* workshop-performances, Georges Aperghis's (1945–) intermedial music theatre, Meredith Monk's (1942–) innovative solo and ensemble vocalizations, Joan La Barbara's (1947–) experimental and virtuosic compositions, Diamanda Galás's (1955–) activist concerts and recordings, Orlando Gough's (1953–) compositions for ballet, theatre and the mixed-genre choir The Shout, or Brandon LaBelle's (1969–) radio and sonic artworks. Such works are designed to create spaces where performed voices go beyond speaking the text or singing the song and towards a territory occupied by less conventional sounds, such as gasps, sighs, sobs, screams, inward breathing and cries – a territory that American composer Michael Edward Edgerton has collectively defined as 'extra-normal voice' (2015, p. xxvii). Each artist practises voice in a distinctive way and in conjunction with varying media and formats; they are united nonetheless by their understanding of voice as material, sonorous and capable of doing much more than accommodating language.

A related concern with non-verbal uses of language is encountered in the work of artists more readily identifiable with theatre making. French writer and director Antonin Artaud (1896–1948), in his manifesto for a theatre of cruelty *The Theatre and Its Double* ([1938] 1958, p. 91), declared that the new theatrical language he propagated extends the voice. It utilizes the vibrations and qualities of the voice. It wildly tramples rhythms underfoot. It pile-drives sounds. It seeks to exalt, to benumb, to charm, to arrest the sensibility. It liberates a new lyricism of gesture which, by its precipitation or its amplitude in the air, ends by surpassing the lyricism of words. It ultimately breaks away from the intellectual subjugation of the language.

Artaud's vision for a sonorous voice, unrestrained by its traditional ties to speech, owes much to his fascination with non-Western performance practices, and could be heard in his radiophonic work *Pour en Finir avec le Jugement de Dieu/ To Have Done with the Judgement of God* (1947). The censored recording, which did not originally air on Radio France because of its obscene and scatological content, tests the boundaries of language through a repetitious, incantatory recitation style, intermingled with haunting screams and guttural sounds. The surrealist, collage-type and rhythmic delivery of textual fragments, alongside the pronounced use of a vocal range much wider than normal speech, renders words almost nonsensical and extends an invitation to encounter Artaud's sonority as breaking through unintelligible speech. Artaud's ideas on voice resonate with earlier and subsequent experiments of the historical avant-garde, from Futurists to Dadaists, who used vocalization as a way to lay bare the limitations of language, 'defamiliarized expression, and blurred the boundaries between speech, music, and noise' (Curtin, 2014, p. 170). Traces of Artaud's thinking can also be found in the development of extended vocal techniques by German voice teacher Alfred Wolfsohn (1896–1962) and the experimental performances devised by his student, Southern African actor Roy Hart (1926–1975), Peter Brook and Ted Hughes's creation of an invented language for the performance *Orghast* (1971, Persepolis), and the detailed training approaches developed by theatre innovators Jerzy Grotowski (1933–1999) and Eugenio Barba (1936–), aimed at rediscovering voice as resonance, impulse and tangible connection between actors and between actors and audiences.

Anti-logocentric efforts, however, have not been the sole domain of actors, directors and pedagogues. For example, Irish playwright Samuel Beckett (1906–1989) created characters that, absurdly, are talking heads stuck in the ground (*Happy Days*, 1961) or, even, just mouths (*Not I*, 1972). In *Waiting for Godot* (1953, Paris/1955, London), Beckett revealed the absurdities of linguistic communication. Near the end of the first Act, the 'waiting' pair of Vladimir and Estragon encounter Pozzo, the master, and Lucky, his servant. Lucky delivers a soliloquy resembling an unintelligible delirium, with no punctuation marks, filled with repetitions and onomatopoeia (words imitating sounds), and culminating in screaming and enforced silence. As Slovenian philosopher of the voice Mladen Dolar (1951–) wrote about Beckett: 'The words have to be deprived of their magic, the meaning has to be subtracted from them so that they become scarce and empty, like senseless sounds, reduced to clichés, dead words within the seemingly living language' (2015, pp. xv–xvi). In musicalizing speech through repetition, alliteration and rhythmicity, this tirade gives prominence to the non-semantic aspects of voiced language and challenges conventional understandings of speaking as meaningful linguistic exchange. Lucky, a mute character for the rest of the play, 'speaks' only when his master instructs him to think (Beckett, 2006, pp. 35–38), but the incoherent sonority of his pouring-out of words is telling of Beckett's critique of the privileging of thinking and speaking over voice. Lucky's voice, much like Electra's, is able to effectively materialize a theatrical reconsideration of voice as equated with articulate speech, not because it counter-privileges voice over speech but because it exposes the tension between the two.

Voicing music

To tap into Electra's performative dynamism and vocal disquiet, Deborah Warner realized that she could not simply ask Fiona Shaw to prepare for the part; the actress had to 'run' it, to perform it with full commitment and energy, even in rehearsals. 'You have to sing it out the whole time'; this is how Warner chose to phrase her understanding of such an approach, and her use of the metaphor of singing built on a concrete comparison: 'In opera, you cannot do an aria without singing it. You either sing it completely, or you don't do it that day' (Poole, Warner & Shaw, 2002). Singing here comes to exemplify an all-out intensity, a type of engagement beyond just delivering lines. Electra's mourning, screaming, noises and exclamations are not singing, nonetheless – at least not most of the time. As Dolar (2006, p. 23) reminded us, Belgian aesthetic semiologist Herman Parret (1938–) would classify such sounds as *prelinguistic* phenomena, as 'presignifying voices ... which appear to tie the human voice to an animal nature'. Such sounds pose a challenge to language and spoken text, because they purportedly pre-exist its development. Singing is *postlinguistic*, a phenomenon requiring further refinement and acculturation; only certain voiced sounds are classified as singing in given cultural contexts and these sounds are not involuntary or intuitive but fulfil an aesthetic function. If shouts, cries, breathing and the similar indicate an unwanted – from the perspective of *logos* – excess of vocality, singing fosters a desired, cultivated (and profitable) vocal excess.

Voice, then, in its theatrical treatment and renditions, is not only normatively linked to text. From musical theatre, vaudeville and burlesque to opera and contemporary 'composed theatre' (see Rebstock & Roesner, 2012), several genres of performance advocate an understanding of voice as rhythm, pitch, melody, and as co-creator of harmonies and polyphonic textures, either in correlation with instruments or without accompaniment; this is voice understood as music. Voicing musically and listening musically to voice in theatre are, however, more complex than merely considering voice as another 'instrument' in a composition, or as another form of expression available to the performer. A case in point can be found in Wolfgang Amadeus Mozart's (1756–1791) opera *Die Zauberflöte/The Magic Flute* (1791, Vienna). The fairytale-like libretto by Bavarian impresario

Emanuel Schikaneder follows a rather simple storyline, interspersed with several side episodes of comedic or adventurous character. Prince Tamino is asked by the Queen of the Night to save her daughter, Pamina, from Sarastro, who has kidnapped her and is holding her in his Temple. Tamino, aided by the birdcatcher Papageno, embarks on the quest to save Pamina, facing trials and discovering in the process that Sarastro is not the malevolent character the Queen of the Night has depicted. The uplifting finale finds Tamino paired up with Pamina, Papageno with another character, Papagena, and the Queen of the Night and her servants banished into eternal night. The plot, filled with references to the rise of freemasonry (Chailley, 1992), has been seen as a metaphor for the struggle between light and darkness, Enlightenment and religion, and, crucially, 'female/nature and male/culture as locked in a struggle for dominance' (Jordanova, 1980, p. 59).

The Queen of the Night is a key protagonist in this struggle and her singing is revelatory of perspectives on female vocality that would later coagulate into full-blown conventions of nineteenth-century Romantic opera. Her two notoriously demanding arias were composed by Mozart with a specific performer in mind: his sister-in-law Josepha Hofer (1758–1819), a soprano with an exceptionally high vocal placement. The first aria, in Act I, is the point in the opera when the Queen asks Tamino to save her daughter, while in the second aria, in Act II, she hands a knife to her daughter and orders her to kill Sarastro. In both cases, the songs have a narrative arc, underscored by the Queen's varying emotions and the shifting logic of argumentation she employs to convince her interlocutors. The poetic metre adapts to accommodate these changes and the music follows suit. Voice here services both music and text and, further, is essential in fusing the two into a coherent musico-textual structure. However, in both instances, there are moments when the voice abandons (or abates) text and presents itself as pure music. These are the fast-paced, ascending series of consecutive notes near the end of the first aria and the recognizable (also from TV commercials) motif of the disconnected, punctuated notes of the second aria that lead to repeated, scale-like interval leaps.

These high-flying vocal feats have been visually mirrored by a production history that has seen the Queen of the Night descending on stage from the ceiling, crossing the space wearing floating veils or occupying a throne at the top of elevated scenographic structures. A more recent counter-history has witnessed an attempt to create a disjunction between the Queen's body and voice and even to eliminate the body generating her well-known vocal music. English director Simon McBurney's (1957–) production of *The Magic Flute* (De Nederlandse Opera, Amsterdam, 2012; English National Opera, London, 2013/2016) was dominated by a sense of flying. Most scenes took place on top of or around a large hovering platform; the agile chorus at times operated bird-shaped props; and Tamino and Pamina, in the final scene, hovered above ground, surrounded by projected visual effects. However, the Queen of the Night (performed by German soprano Cornelia Götz in the performance I attended in London) moved on a wheelchair or walked aided by a cane – her vocal vigour thus creating a stark contrast to her apparent physical frailty. In the 2000–2001 production at the Opéra National de Paris, by Swiss director Benno Besson (1922–2006), French vocalist Natalie Dessay (1965–) resembled a Beckett character as she sang the first aria immobile and covered to the neck inside a mountainous fabric. Are such approaches deliberate attempts at restricting the body in favour of voice? Do they perhaps constitute a form of onstage irony, openly admitting that in such famed moments of vocal exuberance the singer cannot but be perceived as nothing more than a voice? Or do they, consciously or not, continue a long tradition of male authors and interpreters regulating female singing – by just acknowledging it *as mere singing* but not as an activity deeply engaging a body?

A similar tension is inherent in the opera singer's technique. The concrete physical adjustments and the reorganization of the full body necessitated by operatic voicing need not be evident in vocal production, which is expected to sound effortless and freed of strain. For example, the Queen's demandingly-athletic coloratura (singing characterized by florid vocal runs) brings the singers well above their lower, speaking range – called the 'chest register' – and into the highest regions of what is known as the 'head register', the lighter voice beyond everyday speaking tones. However, one of the principal concerns for the singer (see Stark, 1999, pp. 58–73; Miller, 2000) is to achieve a voice quality that blends elements from both registers and to balance a forceless, imperceptible use of the transitional notes between the registers – the points where a non-trained singer or speaker 'breaks'. On the one hand, the singer needs a solid, painstakingly acquired technique to negotiate the taxing vocal tasks performed by her body but, on the other, the voice needs to sound effortless, mellifluous, ethereal.

More than sound?

This appearance/disappearance of the body producing the voice – particularly in the case of female bodies – is a critical issue when discussing voices partaking in musical performance and has preoccupied a series of musicologists. French feminist critic Catherine Clément (1939–), in her idiosyncratic and influential *Opera, or the Undoing of Women* ([1979] 1988), used a blend of personal observation and analysis of mainly nineteenth-century pieces to posit that 'on the opera stage women perpetually sing their eternal undoing' (1988, p. 5). Despite the seemingly fortunate bearing of women in the operatic canon as the foci of its stories or as admired vocalists, their singing is instigated by plots that guide them either to their compliance to patriarchal expectations of marriage and domestication or to their demise. Clément summarized this treatment of operatic women succinctly: 'they suffer, they cry, they die' (1988, p. 11). In this sense, their vocalisms are not just a venerated form of musical expression; they are also a means to an end. They are literally a swan song of their exceptional standing on the operatic stage and they engender both a preamble and a step to their obliteration. Clément's strategy is to look more closely at the texts, the libretti, in an attempt to un-sing the vocal fate of these heroines. Her 'unsinging' of *The Magic Flute*, for example, offers a reading of the plot as investigating the emergence of the bourgeois family: the parents are irreconcilably divorced; the daughter attains her coming of age at the price of symbolically killing the Queen/mother; and the father's order prevails. Much of the criticism subsequently levelled at Clément focuses on her methodology, nevertheless; in a genre where music plays such a paramount role and lyrics are often distorted to the point of incomprehension for the sake of intricate voicing, why examine the *texts* to advance a feminist critique?

American musicologist and historian Carolyn Abbate (1956–) has contended that, if we are to find a possibility for the radical liberation of female voice in opera, we should not be looking exclusively at the text – and not necessarily at the music, either. The music of the widely performed operas is more frequently than not composed by male composers, after all, and could be seen as another type of structure or 'system' that delimits and contains voice. It is not only that this music is 'authored' by male artists, I would add; the relation between text and voice-as-singing comes with its own histories and presuppositions. Aristotle, for example, again in his *Poetics*, construed that tragedy originated from the dithyramb (songs in praise of Dionysus) and comedy from phallic songs, and that this development – effected over time through the innovations of poets – was an 'enhancement' (1995, p. 43). In his 'evolutionary' scenarios, not only does animal-sounding voice transform into political discourse and non-signifying voice into intelligible speech, but also singing is 'promoted' to poetic text. More recently, British singer and researcher John Potter, whose books *Vocal Authority: Singing Style and Ideology* (1998) and *A History of Singing* (2012, with Neil Sorrell) have contributed much to the study of the historical development of singing and of its stylistic variation, also argued for 'a logocentric articulation of musical style: all changes in style relate in some way to the presentation of text' (1998, p. 193). It is not, then, that both music and text have been conceived primarily as logocentric structures (imposing anti-voice strictures), but that in Western thinking text is either the privileged end-point or the stylistic dictator of singing. As Tamino enters Sarastro's Temple, a priest (interestingly called The Speaker in the original libretto) warns him against the Queen's claims: 'Ein Weib tut wenig, plaudert viel' (Freyham, 2009, p. 219). 'A woman does little, [but] chatters a lot': audiences may have just heard the Queen's astounding first aria, but her singing is promptly reduced to speech – purposeless, thoughtless, 'womanly' chattering, for that matter.

To return to Abbate, her musicology proposes a move beyond text and music. Her work points to the fact that, despite the patriarchal connotations of composition and writing, in performance audiences are still confronted with the unique voices of individual singers. On stage, the singers' distinct bodies and distinct voices are co-creators. They assume agency comparable to that of the authors and can subvert any fixed meaning allegedly residing in the music and text. Abbate called this process 'envoicing': 'Author politics in music are thus in great measure also performer politics' (1993, p. 236). In her later book *In Search of Opera* (2001), Abbate stressed that the Queen's second aria is the first to present the singer with these specific technical demands and, as a result, the first to make audiences listen to classical singing in this way: 'with this technical departure, an unprecedented voice comes into being, one with no capacity for melodic conjunction. In this – and not in any simple loss of words – voice metamorphoses into an impossible device, a wind instrument unknown in 1791, unknown ever since' (2001, p. 92). Singing, particularly at points when text is abandoned and when music reconfigures what is vocally possible – singing that is at the edge of its cultural and aesthetic contexts, that is – can firmly anchor voice in the presence of performance. And because this presence, in opera at least, typically involves material bodies as both voicers and listeners, singing can generate new potentials for how these bodies – their genders, their attached normative expectations, or their resistance to any pre-existing structures – are understood and experienced through voice.

Although, or precisely because, singing is seen as a highly acculturated, postlinguistic phenomenon, it can prompt its listeners to actively interrogate these very same cultural constraints imposed on the bodies producing it. This potential is not the exclusive territory of one historical period and one performance genre. Contributors to

Leslie C. Dunn and Nancy A. Jones's collection *Embodied Voices: Representing Female Vocality in Western Culture* (1994) revealed the complex relationship between female voicing and physical bodies in case studies ranging from Finnish folk lamentation to Madonna's pop albums. Dunn's analysis of Ophelia's songs in *Hamlet* (1599/1602), for example, showed that the character's singing should not just be regarded as a customary expression of madness. In a play where sexuality is tirelessly kept at bay and music is mediated and regularized by mostly male listeners, such as Laertes, Polonius and Hamlet himself, Ophelia's singing is an overflow of both uncontained music and eroticism. The male characters' 'anxiety is aroused not only because Ophelia is mad, but also because she is a woman, who becomes even more "Woman" when she sings' (Dunn, 1994, p. 63).

Shifting from early-modern drama to twenty-first-century megamusicals, this interplay of vocality and feminine assertion can be heard in yet another character performing aerial feats: the witch Elphaba in Schwartz and Holzman's *Wicked* (2003, Gershwin Theatre, NYC). The signature song of the show, 'Defying Gravity', comes at the end of Act I, right in the middle of a plot that is largely a prequel to *The Wizard of Oz*. The story explores the opposing worldviews, conflicts and developing friendship between green-skinned Elphaba (soon to be known as the Wicked Witch of the West) and Glinda (later becoming the Good Witch of the South). Just before this scene, Elphaba has discovered that the Wizard is not all he feigned to be. As a result, she decides to leave behind all conventional expectations – encapsulated in

Glinda's character – and performs a successful spell on the broomstick on which she will fly away. The song, first performed by American singer Idina Menzel (1971–), culminates in a non-verbal exclamation, but, unlike the Queen of the Night's vocalisms, the singing is almost entirely text-based and no balance between head and chest registers is attempted. On the contrary, for the final section, the singer brings her speaking register forcibly higher than normal by pushing her belting to laboriously demanding high notes. In the contemporary aesthetics of pop and rock musicals, the singing quality of belting is 'the vocal equivalent of situations and emotions "in extremis" and can be used to express a range of heightened feelings' (Kayes, 2004, p. 156). In the case of belting, the body does not emerge through a letting go of speech but is foregrounded in the audible exertion of the vocal physiology. In her book *Changed for Good*, American musical theatre scholar Stacy Wolf also began her feminist analysis of *Wicked* precisely by attending to this moment of 'ecstatic determination' (2001, p. 3). Wolf's interpretation of the relationship between Glinda and Elphaba as a 'queer romance' (2001, p. 201) renders the cry at the end of the song into both a powerful statement of feminine independence and an obstacle to the implicit romance that will be partially resolved in the characters' final duet 'Changed for Good'.

From the Queen of the Night to Elphaba and from Clément and Abbate to Dunn, Jones and Wolf, feminist perspectives on female characters' singing have listened to their voices as powerful agents towards renegotiating a bodily politics of assertion and affirmative pleasure. Such feminist critiques of operatic and musical theatre vocalization have been instrumental in reminding aficionados, scholars and music-theatre goers of the potential of embodied communication in performance, its ability to subvert textual and musical meaning, and the close ties of voice not only to language but also to physicality. The point could be pushed further, nevertheless. Not all bodies and voices correspond to each other in the seamless way implied in the suggestion that (female) bodies override (male) authorial regulation. One case defying such commonplace classifications is the male falsettist, a male singer voicing in the upper part of their register. Male falsettists produce a sound that in some repertoires could be heard as an 'imitation of the female vocal sound' (Miller, 1996, p. 133). American counter-tenor and musicologist Bradley Fugate has shown that such imitation, depending on the historical context and the musico-theatrical genre, can serve either to reinforce patriarchal views of femininity or to advance the cause for a more tolerant understanding of the complex intersections of bodies, sexes, music and gender. He also admitted, however, that: 'A falsettist's vocal gender is misleading to the average listener, which is why composers throughout history have used the voice type to mimic females on stage – predominantly in musical comedy' (Fugate, 2006, p. 2).

In the Kander/Ebb/Fosse musical *Chicago* (1975, 46th Street Theatre, NYC), which centres on the lives and crimes of 1920s female murderers and the press frenzy surrounding them, one of the lead reporters is Mary Sunshine. The character's solo song 'A Little Bit of Good' is written in the falsetto range and, in both the original Broadway and West End productions as well as the 1990s revivals, has been portrayed by male vocalists. The end of the number sees the character revealing the male performer under the wig, costume and make-up, in a Brechtian wink of the eye to the audience. As heard in recordings of Michael O'Haughey's original performance in NYC and more recent documentation, this is a comedic moment for many spectators. Given the character's influence on the press (an unusual feat for women of the period) and the production's admitted connection to vaudeville (a performance tradition conducive to the staging of LGBTQ identities), such laughter is not necessarily condescending or degrading. It could be heard as the sound of gradual acceptance of alternatives to gender stereotypes or, at least, as an acknowledgement of their constructed nature and the ability of performance to aspire to their de-construction. Yet, audiences never get to hear the voice of the 'uncovered' performer and/or character. Is the 'little bit of good *in* everyone', in this case, unrelated to voice, which is traditionally conceived as the expression of *inner* truth or the self? Is voice presented here as mere *externality*? Answers are partly subject to the performer's choice and agility. The role can be sung either in a fully resonant, 'female-like' register or in a more ambivalent, 'male-sounding-female' tone; either choice can directly undermine stereotypical associations of voice quality with binary gendered identities. Depending on the voicing, and the way it is perceived, Mary Sunshine's voice can be understood as 'misleading' and concealing her internality until the moment of revelation or as bolstering, throughout the performance, a powerful tension between a definitive visual clue (female-looking costume and posture) and an uncomfortable, not-easily-locatable sound.

Such undetermined perceptions of the singing voice have been tackled in different ways by those proposing alternatives to a supposedly homogenous community of listeners. Wolf's study of *Wicked* led her to examine comments in online fora with an ethnographer's curiosity. The example of the multiple readings of Elphaba's cry as fearlessness, rage or laughter goes to show that girl fans can actively reappropriate this 'intensely emotional, diva-like sound' and 'project self-possession onto Elphaba/actor as she sings' (Wolf, 2001, p. 226). In his almost poetic book *The Queen's Throat: Opera, Homosexuality, and the Mystery of Desire* (1993), American critic Wayne Koestenbaum (1958–) elaborated on the significance of operatic singing, and particularly the diva's song, for queer and gay listeners. In his view, the singers can become vehicles for expressing the desires contained and repressed into the gay throat, muted within heteronormative culture. In the performance of operatic singing, Koestenbaum found the possibility to connect to a voice that is 'willing to be thrown, to disguise its source, to hurl itself out of sex-and-gender' (1993, p. 164) and a larynx that 'can embody male and female characteristics, or neither' (1993, p. 161). Unsurprisingly, in Koestenbaum's analysis, too, this possibility is intensified when the voice breaks away from text, music and plot.

A related understanding of voice-as-music was postulated by French historian and sociologist of psychoanalysis Michel Poizat (1947–2003) in his study *The Angel's Cry: Beyond the Pleasure Principle in Opera* (1992). Poizat's 'target' listener, however, is not the girl musical theatre fan or the gay opera-goer; it is the opera fan. Poizat extends Lacan's understanding of voice as an object of desire, as bound to a never-satisfied attempt to return to the infant's state of oneness with the mother, when the baby's cry was not yet interpreted as having specific meaning and when the baby was yet to discover that it was a separate self from the mother responding to the cry (Poizat, 1992, pp. 99–106; this Lacanian analysis of voice would receive its fullest treatment by Dolar in his 2006 *A Voice and Nothing More*). In asking what is the particular type of emotional attachment to a voice that the opera fan experiences, Poizat also found in the operatic 'cry' an answer. The 'cry' can return the listener to this almost infantile state of pure pleasure, as it manifests itself 'unmediated by any system of representation whatsoever' (1992, p. 78). Conceivably achievable or not, this attempt to take 'pure' pleasure in and through voice reveals, once again, its elusiveness. If voice challenges speech and text when it appears as non-signifying sound, then it also challenges music when experienced less as an aesthetic form and more as a reminder of the body producing it and as a mediator between bodies. The Queen of the Night's melismas are not only an attempt to circumvent textuality and patriarchal plots or to imagine new musical possibilities. Her voice, emanating from a body and engaging different bodies-listeners in remarkably divergent ways, matters precisely because of its materiality.

Bodies voicing

Another way, then, to tackle the problem that is a voice, and the even more pressing problems it raises when present in performance, is through the body involved in its making. The type of eroticism implied or expressly invoked in the connection between singers and auditors by Koestenbaum or Poizat is predicated on acknowledging the bodily attributes of voicing and its associated pleasures. One of the first to recognize the body within voice as positive, emancipatory and delivering an 'individual thrill' was French semiotician and critic Roland Barthes (1976, p. 183). In 'The Grain of the Voice', an essay that found wide applicability in studies of popular music, Barthes (1915–1980) proposed that when listening to singing, two orders co-exist and compete with each other: namely, the *pheno*-song – which is the 'surface' of the song, the language, the formal codes of composition and style – and the *geno*-song – which is the materiality of the singer's vocal production. For instance, a voicer of *lieder* (originally, German art songs) could opt for enunciating all the sounds properly and for following slavishly and diligently all the rules and regulations of the musical genre. A second performer, however, might allow the personal shaping of their vocal anatomy to alter and affect the 'correct' version. This is not *a* throat vibrating and *a* mouth fashioning the song; it is *the* particular singer's throat and mouth displacing 'the fringe of contact between music and language' (Barthes, 1976, p. 181). For this sense of the 'body in the voice as it sings' – akin to 'the hand as it writes, the limb as it performs' – Barthes coined the term 'the grain of the voice' (1976, p. 188). In many ways, Barthes drew on observations made by Bulgarian-French critic and philosopher Julia Kristeva (1941–). In her *Revolution in Poetic Language* ([1974] 1984), Kristeva distinguished between phenotext, the structured version of language, and genotext, a more open space of possibilities found in the ambiguous use of words in poetry, its atypical syntax and rhythmical qualities. For Kristeva, this distinction also had affinities with developmental psychology. Before acquiring language and entering the realm of the *symbolic*, the child lives in the realm of the *semiotic*, characterized by physical proximity to the mother's body and non-linguistic sounds and rhythms as the key modes of communication (see Kristeva's *Desire in Language*, 1980). For both Barthes and Kristeva, there is always a trace of the body in voicing, and this trace is a rupture from within language, an effort to work against words and towards unity, sonority and enjoyment.

Tuning in to the body-in-the-voice, however, does not guarantee that this body is not still a generic and generalized body, a body in the abstract. As shown in the previous section, voicing bodies incorporate complex gendered histories and are constructed both by their physiologies and by the ideologies in which they partake. But even when they embody a call to resist these ideologies – as in the liberatory possibilities Abbate, Clément or Kristeva found in alerting listeners to gender, sexuality and sensual materiality – they can also perpetuate a binary logic between male/female, text/sound, language/rhythm, or music/body. This, in turn, can prove counterproductive in accounting for the specificity of bodies that do not sit neatly within such polar oppositions – as in the case of the male falsettist. Another productive way forward is to listen intersectionally to gender, race, ethnicity and class in order to 'account for multiple grounds of identity when considering how the social world is constructed' in and through these bodies (Crenshaw, 1991, p. 1245). Abbate, for example, found in the performances of (white) female opera singers the potential for envoicing. In contrast, when listening intersectionally to the categories of gender and race, it is possible to note that some American musicals – from *Hairspray* (2002, Neil Simon Theatre, NYC) to *The Color Purple* (2005, Broadway Theatre, NYC) – despite purporting to give voice to black women, may frequently de-voice them by shoehorning them into the trope of the 'big black lady' song. The affective power of such voicing may celebrate expressive traits of gospel and blues traditions, communicate lyrics advancing a critique of black oppression or present the singer with a 'show-stopper', but it can simultaneously capitalize on the stereotype of the caring but larger-than-life black lady. As American director Dan Dinero has observed, 'rather than diversifying Broadway musical theatre, big black lady songs marginalize black women, assigning them a limited role' and thereby reaffirm 'Broadway's existence as the Great *White* Way' (2012, p. 30, original emphasis). Race and ethnicity, however, have been mostly associated in performance studies with visuality: 'The concept of race [...] uses the look of a person as an indicator of expectations of background, history, status, and behaviour. [...] Together, these elements *racialize* the everyday act of looking' (H. Young, 2013, p. 5, original emphasis). To talk about racialization rather than race is to point to the social processes and the means by which race comes into being as a category in the first place. Are, then, these techniques and mechanisms of racialization only visual? What about voices as vectors of racialization? How can we also *listen* to the 'sonic color-line', the 'aural dimension of race' (Stoever, 2015, p. 100)? And how can it be heard intersectionally?

In performance, the interplay of voiced identities can be revelatory of deeply entrenched ideological stances. Importantly, it can also provoke us to listen through the apparent naturalness and cohesion of identity categories. The opening number of Lin-Manuel Miranda's musical *Hamilton* (2015, The Public Theatre, NYC), narrating the life of Founding Father Alexander Hamilton (1757–1804), is an exposition of the plot sung by most of the ensemble. The cast, comprising American actors of African, Latino and Asian descent, is purposefully anachronistic in its ethnic diversity (Piepenburg, 2012), and the style of delivery draws on contemporary hip-hop idioms. This is both a visually playful reminder of the dialectics of inclusion and exclusion in the writing of history but also a subversive comment on how belonging can be articulated through sound. Some of the actors have elements of Afro-American or Puerto Rican accent in their voicing while others, including Miranda himself, sound mostly 'generically' American or any variation in their speech has more to do with regionality and adhesion to the musical style rather than ethnicity. These contradictions and the co-presence of standardized and accented speech tread the thin line between subsuming, on the one hand, every articulated difference into the commonalities that make all accents recognizably American and, on the other, making audible the tensions in the very making of 'the' American sound as multiple and heterogeneous.

Turning to the UK, the vocal landscape of Alecky Blythe and Adam Cork's verbatim musical *London Road* (2011, National Theatre, UK) explored the intersection of regionality and class. Blythe collected testimonies around the 2006 serial murders of female prostitutes in Ipswich and based her script on transcribed interviews with residents of the local London Road. Cork's vocal lines maintained much of the inflections and particularities of spoken delivery and, in this way, the speech-song voiced by the actors, despite a degree of personal variation, located them geographically in Suffolk. At the same time, both the linguistic and phonetic components of these song-texts – both what they 'said' and how they 'said' it – markedly rooted these utterances in a working class environment. The final scene may find the residents celebrating and reaffirming their cohesion as a neighbourhood, but the voices of the surviving sex workers, although also perceivably local, are still excluded from this particular social horizon, its values and its definition of community. Earlier on, debbie tucker green's play

Random (2008, Royal Court, UK) examined the stabbing of a black teenager in London and its impact on his family. In this case, voice was even more decidedly bodied. A single actress, Nadine Marshall in the original production, spoke all four characters (Sister, Brother, Mum, Dad). Her vocal virtuosity adapted for different genders, ages and versions of belonging: Mum's speech, for example, was more recognizably Afro-Caribbean while Sister sounded South London. Still, the voicing of four *character* voices by one *performing* voice questioned how 'random' such incidents can be for bodies occupying the same intersections of marginalized identities within the categories of class, ethnicity, race and gender – and are therefore more vulnerable to violence. The embracing of such non-generic voices is a reminder not only of the complex relationship between bodies and voices in performance but also of the assumptions and expectations audiences can impart on these bodies and voices. A reviewer of *Random*, for example, remarked: 'My only complaint [...] is that at first Nadine Marshall's strongly-accented delivery isn't always audible to those more familiar with RP English' (Spencer, 2008). For an unnamed, suspiciously 'general' audience, voice should have been equally 'general'. This expectation to hear voice as non-ethnic, class-unspecific and de-racialized is in fact an expectation to eradicate the body that originates it and silence its diverse origins.

Training voices: embodying more than technique?

To regulate the way voices sound and to privilege some versions of voicing over others is to embed voice in power structures that define who (and what) has the right to be heard. This tendency to discipline voicing is not only present in the act of listening to voices on stage. Mainstream voice training in highly acclaimed conservatories, for example, tends to rely on a monolithic choice of canonical texts and the teaching of an idealized, 'cleaned-up' version of English (Received Pronunciation). These strategies, however, may inadvertently perpetuate 'dysconscious racism' – that is, 'an uncritical mindset that does not challenge the norms and privileges of a dominant culture' (Ginther, 2015, p. 42). To run counter to such dysconscious silencing and erasures, it is urgent to observe, then, that in theatre there is an added level of bodily sedimentation that affects voicing. Unlike Cavarero's philosophical scene, where a uniquely bodied voice encounters another uniquely bodied voice, in performance, prior to entering the theatrical stage, actors' and singers' voices have, more frequently than not, been trained (and/or rehearsed). If Clément and Abbate's female singer was culturally and socially 'trained' into being a 'feminine' body that is only permitted to voice in designated places within operatic plots and music, this same body-voice also underwent years of professional training, a training that fundamentally altered how the performer used, perceived and experienced her voicing body. In this sense, such voicing bodies are doubly trained and audiences listen dually to the balancing and antagonisms between the actor's individual voice (Maria Callas *as a singular and unrepeatable voice*, for example) and the training it embodies (Maria Callas *as a trained opera singer*). It is for this reason that when attending to the construction of vocal bodies, it is particularly useful to consider them not only in performance but also, crucially, during and as parts of systems of voice pedagogy.

From the middle of the twentieth century onwards, the predominant approach to speech training, in the UK and the US at least, has been what could be inclusively described as the training of the 'natural/free' voice. The approach has been mainly developed by the first voice director of the Royal Shakespeare Company, Cicely Berry (1926–), voice teacher Kristin Linklater (1936–), who has mostly been affiliated with US companies and universities, and Patsy Rodenburg (1953–), the Head of Voice for the Guildhall School of Music and Drama and voice coach for the National Theatre in London. Despite the distinctiveness of each pedagogue's teaching (see Martin, 1991, pp. 171–179), Berry, Linklater and Rodenburg – through their extensive teaching and coaching, a series of highly influential publications and a lineage of voice specialists they trained – have generated a permeating paradigm of voice work. Its key tenets are that aspiring actors arrive at the training with voices that have been inhibited by a restrictive culture and education that polices *free* voicing as well as with psychological histories and bodily habits that also impact on vocal expression (Berry, [1973] 2000, pp. 11–17; Linklater, [1976] 2006, pp. 19–25; Rodenburg, 2000, pp. 9–13). To redress these effects, students should undergo the de-structuring process of eliminating excess tension through relaxation and self-awareness exercises. Progressively, this new awareness should lead to a re-discovery of the trainees' *natural* voice and its subsequent development through principles based on the healthy use of their vocal physiology. The aim is to achieve their full potential when using their (now resonant, efficient and sustainable) voices – primarily to speak poetic text, at least during training. However, this way of thinking about bodies and voices in training has triggered critiques by a recent generation of practitioners and scholars, especially regarding its ideological impact (Knowles, 1996; Werner, 1996; Inchley, 2015, pp. 49–57), the ways it structures the trainees' perception of their embodied selves (Thomaidis, 2013; Schlichter, 2014) and its incompatibility with ways of working with voice across cultures (McAllister-Viel, 2007, 2015) or with diverse groups of students (Ginther, 2015). This model of freedom/naturalness may have proved extremely helpful for actors working, or hoping to work, on mainstream stages, but, given its wide circulation and influence, it can also be hard to discern that, although it sounds convincingly 'natural', it is a *construction* of the natural, a way of thinking about what voices and bodies 'naturally' do. Is it necessary for a voicing body to conceive of itself as having been *afflicted* by culture? Rather than live through a ruptured personal history, divided between pre-training restriction/tension and post-training freedom, could the trainee's body experience a continuous history? Are scientifically informed models of vocal anatomy, interwoven with occasionally non-specialist psychology, the only way towards professional voicing?

An example of an alternative way to practise the voicing body is to go beyond its confined boundaries as a singular entity and think of it in relational terms. From Jerzy Grotowski's (1933–1999) Theatre Laboratory and Włodzimierz Staniewski's (1950–) Gardzienice to Grzegorz Bral's (1961–) Piesn Kozla/Song of the Goat and Jarosław Fret's (1971–) Teatr ZAR, there is a varied lineage of Polish theatre practitioners, trainers and companies who develop their performances through extensive vocal training and treat directing as an activity deeply related to composition. However, the way voice is practised does not build on a conceptualization of the trainee's body as singular, self-contained and mechanistically efficient. Russian philosopher Mikhail Bakhtin's distinction between the bourgeois, individualized body and the grotesque, interactive and responsive body encountered in carnivals and popular medieval celebrations was influential in how Staniewski formulated the principles of his training (Bakhtin, 1984, pp. 303–367). Since 1976, Staniewski's company, Gardzienice, has lived and trained in the village of the same name in the Polish borderland. During the 1970s and 1980s, the company organized expeditions to villages (or abroad) and learnt 'songs that are strongly connected to a given people, or a given tradition' through gatherings with locals (Staniewski & Hodge, 2004, p. 67). Much of the training happened in the rural and reflected Staniewski's ecological concerns and desire to de-urbanize actor training. The vocal pedagogy in this instance combines acrobatic physicality with complex polyphonic singing and is premised on the principle of mutuality, the interaction and cooperative trust between partners. Voice in this way is trained as impulse between performers, as call and response, and as part of the intricate sonic textures of folk songs which necessitate a sensitive cultivation of listening to the resonances, vocalizations and harmonies of each explored tradition. Emphasis, then, is placed not on the individual but on the ensemble, training hours are long and demanding, and much of the singing is highly energetic and underscored by athletic movement. If the natural/free approach to voice requires an attention to the actor's natural self, freed idiosyncrasy and healthy physiology, this strand of work advocates voicing bodies that are responsive, co-present, porous and radically intersubjective.

Even the seemingly undisputed concept of anatomically correct voicing could be re-examined through instances of vocal practice that do not espouse that model. Korean *pansori* is a form of epic storytelling, incorporating both sung and spoken parts and voiced by a solo singer. In the traditional set-up – as crystallized in the eighteenth and nineteenth centuries – the singer is accompanied only by a drummer, and undertakes the task of giving voice to all characters in performances that can last several hours. To be able to memorize the narratives, which conventionally are transmitted through a master-trainee system of oral pedagogy, and to embody the qualities inextricably associated with *pansori* voicing, the singer undergoes years of training. An outcome of this training is that the singer's voice exhibits hard glottal attacks, pharyngeal tension and a sound that is restricted and forceful, as *pansori* aesthetics 'prizes perseverance rather than ease' (Park, 2003, p. 157). Early accounts of training regimes mention trainees spitting blood when vigorously exercising their voices (Pihl, 1994, p. 105) and research suggests that, in fact, the vocal folds acquire permanent nodes that are responsible for the recognizably husky and sorrowful sound of *pansori* (Kang, 1999; McAllister-Viel, 2007). *Pansori* is not a rarity in embracing such an approach; other East Asian performance traditions, such as Okinawan music, also postulate their vocal aesthetics on a training that breaks or 'splits' the voice (Gillan, 2017). If the concept of 'healthy' voicing in mainstream UK/US pedagogies is predicated on the cultivation of adaptable vocal folds, *pansori* and other forms of performance and training permanently modify vocal anatomy beyond what Western laryngologists might suggest is 'risky' and irreversibly 'damaging'. In other words, even what tends to be presented as a universally acceptable vocal ideal could be probed further in relation to practices that perceive bodies-in-training in ways incompatible with prevalent ways of thinking about voice pedagogy.

Listening intersectionally to the gender, race, ethnicity, regionality and class of voicing bodies as well as thinking of non-normative conceptualizations of the trained vocal body – such as the intersubjective or the 'unhealthy' one – present the bodily constitution of the vocal as both processual and ideological. How much any category of identity can be heard through voice and the extent to which the voicing physiology is to be adapted through training are dependent not only on the biological capacities of voicing but also on the expectations, both aesthetic and social, placed on it by listeners – be it listening audiences or listening teachers. In 1975, Serbian performance artist Marina Abramović (1946–) performed the piece *Freeing the Voice* in Belgrade. The title of the performance might resonate with Linklater's first book, *Freeing the Natural Voice*, even though their approaches are diametrically opposed. Lying on her back, with her neck and head tilted back, Abramović shouted continually until she lost her voice. The intention was to test the connection between vocality and physicality and to achieve a type of cleansing of the bodymind through screaming (Richards, 2010, p. 16). However, particularly when watching the documentation of the performance today, it is hard not to hear in the piece the politics of assigning inarticulacy and pre-linguistic excess to the body of a female and (for the international installations of the piece) foreign artist, or not to compare it to Berry, Rodenburg or Linklater's versions of vocal freedom. Gardzienice's surplus vocality, *pansori*'s permanently modified larynxes, and Abramović's tense, gradually exhausted and hoarse voice are particularly useful provocations towards reassessing received understandings of voice. Such examples make audible the significant ideological and physical labour that goes into vocal production – and into making this labour palatably invisible in the case of predominant or idealized versions of voicing.

Voices beyond bodies

The presence of the trained body within a voice can also be an unwelcome occurrence. In 2007/2008, Canadian director Robert Lepage devised *Lipsynch* (Northern

Stage, Newcastle-upon-Tyne, UK/Salle Pierre Mercure, Montréal, Canada), a nine-hour, episodic performance exploring various iterations of voicing, from news broadcasting and cosmopolitan multilingualism to temporary loss of speech due to post-operative aphasia. In the third segment of the show, Marie, a former jazz singer who now works as a voice-over artist, decides to have an old family Super 8 film dubbed. The silent sequence is of her father wishing young Marie and her sister a merry Christmas. The male actor hired for the job treats this as any other professional engagement: in the first take, he makes the father sound like a smooth, crooning commercial and in his second try, a cartoonish voice is attempted. Listening from the recording booth, Marie exclaims in frustration, 'His voice is too trained!' If dubbing is taken as the craft of matching the movement of onscreen lips to sounds voiced in the studio ('visual/optical synchrony') or of expressing a faithful version of the original content of a scene through translated words ('content synchrony'), then the actor's delivery in this case would score high; however, one aspect that listeners of dubbed voices cannot overlook – and research indicates that they *can* overlook minor asynchronies in lip movement – is 'audio/acoustic' synchrony, the correspondence between the vocal 'type' of the character, their timbre and prosody, and the actor's voice (Whitman-Linsen, 1992, p. 19; see also Kreiman & Sidtis, 2013, pp. 382–384). It is not only that Marie perhaps hopes for the impossibility of hearing her deceased father's voice again. It is also that the voice or voices she has at her disposal are versions that do not even begin to meet the minimum expectation of plausibility.

With the proliferation of voices transmitted through telephones, radios and screen media or recorded and reproduced by phonographs, LPs, cassettes, CDs and digital files, expectations of what is to be heard as vocally credible, natural or authentic have been in constant flux. In many ways, *Lipsynch* came at the end of the more-than-a-century-old rethinking of aurality instigated by the advent of modernity and the technologization of voice, and proposed to explore voice in 'its many manifestations, declensions and implications through different procedures that convey and reproduce it' (Ex Machina, 2015). Some of the most nuanced storylines in the production examined the complex intersections between bodies, voices, identities and technologies. Apart from Marie, there is Jackson, a Glaswegian detective aided by a speaker identification specialist in the comparison of vocal samples from a radio interview and a voice message; Mary (portrayed by male actor John Cobb), the old speech therapist who is videotaped while trying to remember specific words during an interview; and Tony, a BBC radio broadcaster who altered his native Mancunian accent to conceal his roots and family past. In these instances, mediatized voices and physical bodies do not completely align to form a unified whole, and much dramaturgical impetus is derived from these misalignments. English literary/cultural scholar Steven Connor (1955–), in *Dumbstruck: A Cultural History of Ventriloquism*, proposed that, apart from the physical body that produces a voice, there is another body that is produced by the expectations vested in the voice by the listener. Connor named this the 'vocalic body':

> The vocalic body is the idea – which can take the form of dream, fantasy, ideal, theological doctrine, or hallucination – of a surrogate or secondary body, a projection of a new way of having or being a body, formed and sustained out of the autonomous operations of the voice. [...] The same is true of any object given a voice; the doll, the glove puppet [...]. Our assumption that the object is speaking allows its voice to assume that body, in the theatrical or even theological sense, as an actor assumes a role, or as the divinity assumes incarnate form; not just to enter and suffuse it, but to produce it. (2000, pp. 35–36)

A way to think about Connor's vocalic body is through the example of telephonic conversation. When our interlocutor is unknown, we may imagine their bodily features and ethnic, racial, social or gendered identities. We assign to this particular voice an imaginary body that fits our perception, impressions and guesses. This is a vocalic body, a 'surrogate or secondary body', substituting for the body we have not met. Sometimes, our assumptions may come to be verified by the physical attributes of the voicer, but, on other occasions, they can prove to be misleading (and presumptuous). Marie's exasperation derives precisely from her inability to have her actor recreate a seamless fusion between the filmed body of her father and his vocalic body as she remembers it. The vocalic bodies hopelessly formulated by the actor cannot be annexed to the visual document of her father's body as effective vocal surrogates.

Such slippages, perceived inaccuracies and frictions between bodies and voices, which technological reproduction foregrounded and largely enabled, have been ingrained with widespread fantasies around disembodied voicing and its alleged powers. The first of such powers is preservation, immortalization and re-performance. Thomas Edison (1847–1931) anticipated this when introducing the phonograph. One of the ostensible applications of the device was to work as a family record by archiving 'the sayings, the voices, and the *last words* of the dying member of the family' (1878, p. 533, original emphasis). Because recorded voice can outlive its voicer, a reproduction of voice can both act as an invocation of the deceased body and gesture to the futility of any attempt to return voice back to embodiment. German philosopher Theodor Adorno (1903–1969), in his 1928 essay 'The Curves of the Needle', saw a more individualist and egocentric purpose to the whole operation. In listening to the singer's voice as reproduced on the gramophone, the listener reaffirms the possibility of his own preservation in the same way. The bourgeois consumer of recorded voices is self-referentially fascinated with the potential to have his own voice emulated and immortalized. In another passage, Adorno also alluded to another myth linked to recorded vocality: that it is incomplete or that it can throw the completeness of the body out of balance. Perhaps unsurprisingly, this would hold true only for female singers whose gramophoned voices sounded, according to Adorno, 'needy and incomplete' and required 'the physical appearance of the body that carries' them (1990, p. 54). Jim Cartwright's 1992 play *The Rise and Fall of Little Voice* (National Theatre, UK) utilized such anxieties associated with recorded voicing as character-building devices. Little Voice, the introverted main character, plays repeatedly her dead father's collection of records. In doing so, she becomes a masterful impersonator of iconic voices such as Marilyn Monroe and Judy Garland. The LPs act as memorabilia of her father as an avid listener. Little Voice herself, contrasted throughout the play with her extravagant and profligate mother, seems to develop skills in sociability and communication only when mimicking the singers. Adorno's fantasies of the female voice are present here in their extreme materialization; the shy body of Little Voice is overtaken by the recorded voice in an attempt to achieve contact with the lost parent and a sense of full-bodied presence.

The successes and disjunctions in conjoining visual bodies and vocalic bodies have been consistently exploited in film, a medium relying on audio-visual unity for much of its effectiveness. French composer and film theorist Michel Chion (1947–) has further argued that there is a specifically cinematic form of relating voices to bodies, namely the *acousmêtre* (1999, p. 19). The coined term can be translated as *an acousmatic being*, a vocal presence that exists without any visible connection to its source, as is emblematically the case with the voice of computer Hal in Stanley Kubrick's *2001: A Space Odyssey* (1968). Given that the body that could potentially be assigned to the voice of the *acousmêtre* is not visible on screen, the voice, according to Chion (1999, pp. 24–27), acquires almost god-like capabilities. It is experienced as ubiquitously present, able to see and know all, and in possession of limitless powers. Once again, the sounding of a voice without a traceable connection to a body is the source of instability and auditory anxieties related to a loss of control over the voice. Cases of theatrical *acousmêtres* are not as frequent as in cinema, but parts of Chion's analysis could be of relevance. In *Lipsynch*, Jackson, the detective, investigates the suspicious death of Tony, the radio presenter who re-trained his speech to eradicate his accent. Jackson first encounters the female suspect's voice as an acousmatic being, as recorded voice messages that are amplified in the lab and that, by virtue of this amplification and the fact that they come from an unidentified body, bestow a set of powers and control on the unnamed 'criminal'. Ultimately, Jackson will trace the voice back to its source, Tony's prostitute sister who most probably did not commit the crime, and the powers of the disembodied voice will dissipate as soon as her body and voice reunite. This act of 'de-acousmatization' (Chion, 1999, p. 27), of revealing the body to which the voice belongs, results in the instant dilution of the *acousmêtre*'s exceptional agency. For the audience of *Lipsynch*, the first voice sample of the suspect almost certainly gets de-acousmatized before Jackson's discovery. The detective compares the voice messages to an extract from a radio interview with Tony's sister, which we – unlike Jackson – have already watched in a previous scene. This temporal delay between the two de-acousmatizations, the first performed by the audience and the second accomplished by the character/detective, can be a means to free spectators from plot-induced suspense and turn their attention to the ways in which de-acousmatization happens instead. Rather than listening out for the suspect, audiences are invited to listen in to *how* speaker identification is conducted. This is also an invitation to attend to the juxtaposition between a victim who modified his voice to create his radio-disseminated persona and a suspect whose voice is tenaciously consistent – over the phone, on the radio and in live encounters.

This interplay of acousmatization/de-acousmatization in performance can then be less absolute and categorical. For example, in the Wooster Group's rendition of Racine's *Phèdre*, titled *To You, the Birdie!* (2001, The Performing Garage, NYC/Centre Pompidou, Paris), Phaedra's lines were read by Scott Shepherd, the male actor performing Theramenes. In stark contrast to the embodied Phaedra, his microphoned delivery, pitched in a falsetto voice, was monotonous and matter-of-fact. Given his positioning outside the main playing area and the delay in the speaker amplification of the sound, the voice could be perceived as an other-worldly, controlling *acousmêtre* manipulating the action. Yet, it could also be heard as an intentional attempt to fracture and disperse the audience's attention and to highlight the arbitrary logic by which each audience member selected the auditory cues they experienced and interpreted. As practitioner-researcher George Home-Cook noted in *Theatre and Aural Attention*, 'whilst we may be able to see the source to which a given sound supposedly corresponds, we do not always *experience* designed sound as being produced by or at its source' (2015, p. 87, original emphasis). Depending on each audience member's sensorial perspective within the auditorium, technologically mediated voice can reproduce the discourses of immortality, instability, incompleteness and omnipresence with which it has been endowed. Or, it can subversively unmask them as mythologies that can be points of departure but not absolute determinants of the experience. Significantly, it can also alternate between the two approaches as the performance unfolds.

Many voices and voices of the many

To return to the synthesized voice of Margaux in Rimini Protokoll's *Remote Paris*, there is a complex scene that exemplifies both her affinities with and her distance from other acousmatic beings. Halfway through the performance, and just after we have visited Hôpital Saint-Louis, we enter a small chapel. A polyphonic 'Kyrie Eleison' is played through the headphones while we take our seats on the pews. When heard again, Margaux's voice echoes as if reverberating inside a cathedral: 'I am in your midst without being present. There are no portraits of me in here, no sculptures, no symbols. I do not leave any traces. But I am there. Always.' After listing some of the existential questions a church visitor might contemplate, Margaux continues: 'Am I too artificial? Is there something about me that you don't like? That I always know and predict everything? […] Perhaps I have other faces, completely different. I will transform now. I will become Bruno. Bruno is also me, even if he sometimes pretends he is not. Are you ready?' For the next few seconds, the phrase 'I am Margaux' is repeated, gradually mutating into 'I am Bruno.' We now hear a male-pitched voice: 'My name is Bruno. Do not be afraid. Everything is preserved, nothing is lost. But there is also change with me. I am not Margaux. Even if Margaux pretends the opposite.' Like an *acousmêtre*, the voice in *Remote Paris* is always present in our aural field, can witness everything we see even when it appears as a spontaneous happening, and has all the information we need to navigate our way through the urban landscape. It also organizes us into a formation of followers, displays unusual powers of transformation and adopts a theological discourse when referring to itself. It is, however, this self-referentiality that also de-acousmatizes Margaux/Bruno. Margaux and Bruno contradict each other and predict such inconsistencies, and also make no effort to hide their artificiality. We may have no option but to abide by Bruno's guidance if we are to continue in *Remote Paris*, but the expectation of a body – so central to the formation of the *acousmêtre* – has been largely annihilated. This voice is clearly software generated, and, even if, by growing accustomed to Margaux, we may have started invoking a vocalic body for her, her metamorphosis into Bruno undoes our efforts. Moreover, there is a special type of trust developed with Margaux/Bruno over the course of the piece, an intimacy that complicates the top-down obedience claimed by the *acousmêtre*.

Margaux/Bruno pertains to a lineage of experimentations with voice synthesis that, as an aesthetic tool, has found wider applicability in film and music rather than theatre-making. In 1981, American composer-performer Laurie Anderson (1947–) released 'O Superman' (now catalogued in the online Steven Leiber collection of MoMa, NYC), a song where text is overlaid on a harmonic base of a single repeated syllable. The semi-spoken text was inputted, de-composed as audio data, and re-synthesized using a vocoder, a speech synthesis device that, in this process of encoding and decoding voice, renders its sound mechanical and robotic. Not unlike the moment of vocal transfiguration in *Remote Paris*, the voice in 'O Superman' incorporates an answering machine message from the narrator's mother, but, as the song progresses, it transpires that the speaker is someone not known to the narrator. Was the speaker lying at first? Or, is the identity of the speaker transposed and reconstructed during the song? The electronically processed voice manifestly integrates the perspectives of two speakers, but, as sound, it remains uncannily unvaried and immutable. Margaux/Bruno, on the other hand, does not have one homogeneous sound and may state its artificiality, but, in fact, sounds all too human, like a voice intimately whispering in our ears.

Australian sound and intermedia artist Norie Neumark observed that the direct, intimate and seemingly personal character of works such as Canadian artist Janet Cardiff's

(1957–) audio walks or Slovenian artist Igor Štromajer's (1967–) internet operas actually produces an 'authenticity effect' (2010, p. 114). This is not an 'authentic' connection to a body pre-existing the performance; rather, intimacy is generated *during and through the act of listening*, which also produces the 'bodies' with which we become aurally connected. Such production of authenticity and bodily proximity can be facilitated in part by the specific types of listening to voice facilitated by the use of headphones. New Zealander composer and researcher Miriama Young argued in *Singing the Body Electric* that new forms of listening to voice through transportable devices – what she calls 'pod listening' (2015, pp. 158–162) – counter the modern history of alienation between mediated voices and physical bodies and create aural spaces of immediacy between listener and voicer. These spaces, I would add, can be productively explored for their performative possibilities. When attending David Rosenberg and Glen Neath's performance *The Ring* (2013, BAC, London), for example, we were all handed headphones and sat in a circular configuration. Once we were greeted by an actor/character, Michael, the room was plunged into darkness and we were encouraged to move our chairs into a new configuration. As soon as the sound of shuffling about began, I was asked by Michael to stay where I was and, throughout the performance, I was given particular instructions, including executing specific movements. At the end of the narrative, the lights went up to reveal that nobody had in fact moved and, when asked who among us was the 'selected' one, we all raised our hands. The illusion of being personally addressed by the actor's voice was created through binaural recording, which imitates the way sound is perceived differently by the two ears. Paradoxically, while producing an authenticity and personal proximity effect, *The Ring* also led us all towards a *togetherness effect*. Some of us, at least, may have thought that we were singular and alone, but we were also forging a (misguided and involuntary) community of people sharing the deceitful experience of being singular and alone.

What could the role of mediated voice be, then, in the construction of communities? Media anthropologist Charles Hirschkind, when examining the popular practice, among Egyptian Muslims, of listening to cassette sermons, proposed that these recorded voices do not simply impart specific forms of rhetoric: 'The unique musicality of sermon discourse [...] recruits the body' of the listener in its entirety (2006, pp. 13, 25). It is precisely this experience of sensed voice that opens up spaces for a reconsideration of politics not only as discourse (public debate) but, importantly, as affect (bodily participation). This bodily and participatory intertwining of voicing and listening also underpin British electronic composer Matthew Herbert's (1972–) contribution to the Wellcome Trust exhibition 'This Is a Voice' (2016). *Chorus* was an installation asking individual visitors to enter a sound booth and record a single note, which was then added to all previously recorded tones. The assembly of voices formulated in this way could be heard in the physical space but is now also available online, giving listeners the tools to distort, recompose and alter the choral result. The ever-expanding, indeterminate scope of *Chorus* presents voice as malleable material but also highlights the engagement of the listener as the primary parameter that defines how these voices are to be felt and perceived. In both instances, the act of listening to the recorded voice, be it fixed or modifiable, recruits the body of the listener towards wider aesthetic and political collectivities.

American musician and activist Christopher DeLaurenti (1967–) has also developed a strand of work that he defines as 'activist sound' (2015). Using recorded material from protests, such as Occupy Wall Street (2012) or the N30 WTO protests in Seattle (1999), DeLaurenti has created protest symphonies, works both freely downloadable and performed as sound installations. The vocalic bodies heard in these pieces are those of activists. However, DeLaurenti, recording from amidst the protest and manipulating sound only minimally, also foregrounds his bodily presence as the listener who records. Rather than composing an acoustically filtered version of marching and slogans 'from the outside', these pieces draw attention to the very makings of collective voicing, the moments when rallying cries compete with each other. Individual voices interfere with group chanting and different calls and responses collude and expose the unruly, contestatory and processual formation of political consensus and cohesion. In *Notes towards a Performative Theory of Assembly* (2015), Judith Butler argued that bodies that assemble in public spaces speak even before they voice their demands by 'showing up, standing, breathing, moving, standing still' (p. 18). Works such as DeLaurenti's or Herbert's may invite us to consider that the vocalic and listening bodies they invoke also 'take up space' – not necessarily physical – and can enact 'a claim to the political' (p. 17).

Conclusion: from voice to voicing

From speaking text to singing intricate melodies and from the re-enactment of polyphonic traditions to posthuman voicing, voice can be the carrier of language, the sonority of music, the body heard in the sound, a convergence between individuality and community, or an emancipation from pre-determined dependencies on bodily presence and aesthetic expectations. Significantly, at least in performance, voice can simultaneously occupy multiple of these positionalities or elusively translocate between them. In this sense, voice cannot be conclusively and resolutely circumscribed as a fixed entity – although such reductions can always seep into the ways we think or talk about voice. Voice is plural, and, as noted in a recent collaboration with musical theatre scholar Ben Macpherson, 'when seeking to ask what voice *is* [...] there is [...] no definite article: *the* voice does not exist' (Thomaidis & Macpherson, 2015, p. 4, original emphases). In *Gardens Speak* (2014, Artsadmin, London), an immersive sound piece by Lebanese-British artist Tania El Khoury, ten participants lay on garden soil in front of tombstones. The installation referenced the lives of Syrian activists buried now in their home gardens. Each participant listened to an activist's story as reconstructed through interviews with family and friends and then recorded and reproduced in the first person. These voices were both felt, intimate vibrations through the ground and significant (and signifying) testimonies. Their tone was autobiographical, yet they voiced a communal history and had been collectively reassembled by surviving relatives. In sounding unmediatedly personal, each voice could be mis-recognized as singular but was in fact a paradoxical, monophonic chorus. Experienced in this way, *Gardens Speak* was an affective reminder of the plurality that goes into constructing voice *as* singular.

Throughout *Theatre & Voice*, I have discussed multiple ways of listening to such plurality. When experiencing voice, the listener can filter out non-signifying voice in favour of speech (Aristotle), encounter the unique individuality of another embodied being (Cavarero), locate voice within a specific soundscape (Schafer), take pleasure when voice transgresses textual or musical boundaries (Abbate, Poizat, Koestenbaum), listen out for the marked specificity of the individual voicer's 'grain' (Barthes), attest to how voice is produced at the intersections of identity categories (Stoever, Ginther), observe whether its attachment to a body appears synchronized or disjointed (Chion), or imagine a surrogate body that matches the listener's expectations (Connor). Such varied experiences of listening could be complicated even further, because listening is also a culturally and historically situated practice. For example, listeners may resist the reception of voice and make it hard for speakers to reach and persuade them; in other words, the listener's body can be an effective 'obstacle to vocal transmission' – as was frequently the case in early modern England (Bloom, 2007, p. 112). Moreover, listening can be an active process of erasure and silencing. Ethnographer Ana María Ochoa Gautier has shown how, in nineteenth-century Colombia, indigenous sounds, songs, languages and perceptions of voice were gradually colonized and standardized by governors and ethnographers in the process of creating a homogenous nation; listening was proactively 'divesting the voice of unwanted features' (2014, p. 20). To return to theatre, sound designer and scholar Ross Brown has indicated that audiences not only hear voice through an integration of all their senses but that they also hear their own breathing, sounding body – their 'aural body' (2010, p. 2015) – when listening to another. Audiences' sensorial experiences of voice and habits of listening shape what voice is and does in performance, much in the same way that everyday identity-making and performance training or rehearsal shape how voice is produced. The many and proliferative possibilities of listening reveal how active the listener of voices is in defining and deciding how these voices are heard. Not only is voice multiple, it is also heard plurally.

This 'in-between-ness' of voice is particularly powerful when it is not experienced as neat, comfortable or balanced – like the perfectly calculated middle point in a continuum from voicer to listener or a tidy Venn diagram between text and sound, body and language, subjectivity and the political. Voice in performance can bring our attention to the relative and continually contested boundaries between its production and its reception. The unnerving voice of Shaw's Electra, the excess of operatic voice as it breaks through music or text, Abramović's vocal exertion, the implausible dubbing of Marie's father in *Lipsynch*, the unruliness of DeLaurenti's activist voices and Margaux/Bruno's vocal transformation, all propose voice as unresolved or undecided. They are moments when audiences become aware not only of how multiply constructed and performative voice is, but also of their own assumptions and ideas about voice. Because such moments do not subscribe tacitly to embedded assumptions and aesthetic ideas around voice, they expose the making of voice as a process involving both listeners and voicers, their ideological habits, sensory modalities and aesthetic agendas. These are opportunities to radically renegotiate voice, to de-naturalize conventional ideas about something seemingly so familiar and to rethink *voice* not as given or fixed but as the plural, in-between, challenging and generative practice of *voicing*.

further reading

Books that explore theatre and voice and are not how-to publications addressed to practitioners are surprisingly scarce. As a starting point, Inchley and Bloom's monographs are exceptional in their critical approach to voice in contemporary UK playwriting and early modern England respectively. Kimbrough covers much theoretical ground, and, for key philosophical perspectives on voice, read Cavarero, Dolar, Connor and Derrida. Vocal identity is not necessarily discussed as intersectional in these works, but these writings offer some of the most wide-ranging analyses of voice to date. Rich feminist perspectives on vocality have been generated by Abbate, Clément and Kristeva. As an entry point to the discussion of bodies and voices, read 'The Grain of the Voice' by Barthes, and combine this with Poizat, Koestenbaum and Chion, if interested in listening. For perspectives on voice and technology, good starting points are Adorno, Edison, Chion and Hirschkind, while

M. Young's book also includes an appendix of works for electronic voice and interviews with composers. If your interest in voice is geared towards practice, read Berry, Linklater and Rodenburg (spoken text), Kayes (musical theatre), Miller (classical voice), Edgerton (extended voice) and Staniewski and Hodge (musicality) – and also experiment with their exercises. Kreiman and Sidtis have compiled a comprehensive overview of research on vocal production and perception. Potter and Martin provide much needed historical perspective. For a broader discussion of sound and aurality, start with Artaud, Schafer, Brown, Curtin and Home-Cook (and also visit Stoever's blog *Sounding Out!*). For perspectives outside North America and Europe, read Hirschkind, Park, Pihl, Ochoa Gautier and Potter and Sorrell. Having argued for voice as plural, I do tend to return to more multi-vocal works, such as the collections by Dunn and Jones or Neumark, Gibson and van Leeuwen, the special issues in *Performance Research* (MacDonald) and *Studies in Musical Theatre* (Taylor), and journals such as *Voice and Speech Review* or the *Journal of Interdisciplinary Voice Studies*. A readership of theatre professionals may find that the section 'Approaches to Theatre Training: Pillars of Voice Work' of *American Theatre* magazine (January 2010) offers such a polyvocally engaging point of departure.

bibliography

Abbate, Carolyn. *In Search of Opera*. Princeton, NJ: Princeton University Press, 2001.

Abbate, Carolyn. 'Opera; or, the Envoicing of Women'. *Musicology and Difference: Gender and Sexuality in Music Scholarship*. Ed. Ruth Solie. Berkeley, CA: University of California Press, 1993. 225–258.

Adorno, Theodor. 'The Curves of the Needle'. Trans. Thomas Y. Levin. *October* 55 (1990): 48–55.

Aristotle. *Poetics*. Trans. Stephen Halliwell. Cambridge, MA: Harvard University Press, 1995.

Aristotle. *Politics*. Trans. Harris Rackham. Cambridge, MA: Harvard University Press, [1932] 2014.

Artaud, Antonin. *The Theatre and Its Double*. Trans. Mary Caroline Richards. New York, NY: Grove Press, [1938] 1958.

Austin, J.L. *How to Do Things with Words*. Oxford, UK: Clarendon Press, 1962.

Bakhtin, Mikhail. *Rabelais and His World*. Trans. Hélène Iswolsky. Bloomington, IN and Indianapolis, IN: Indiana University Press, 1984.

Barba, Eugenio & Nicola Savarese. *A Dictionary of Theatre Anthropology: The Secret Art of the Performer*. London, UK and New York, NY: Routledge, [1991] 2005.

Barthes, Roland. *Image, Music, Text*. Trans. Stephen Heath. London, UK: Fontana Press, 1976.

Beckett, Samuel. *Waiting for Godot*. London, UK: Faber and Faber, 2006.

Berry, Cicely. *Voice and the Actor*. 2nd ed. London, UK: Virgin Books, [1973] 2000.

Bloom, Gina. *Voice in Motion: Staging Gender, Shaping Sound in Early Modern England*. Philadelphia, PA: University of Pennsylvania Press, 2007.

Brown, Ross. *Sound: A Reader in Theatre Practice*. Basingstoke, UK: Palgrave Macmillan, 2010.

Butler, Judith. *Notes toward a Performative Theory of Assembly*. New York, NY: Routledge, 2015.

Cavarero, Adriana. *For More than One Voice: Toward a Philosophy of Vocal Expression*. Trans. Paul A. Kottman. Stanford, CA: Stanford University Press, 2005.

Chailley, Jacques. *The Magic Flute Unveiled: Esoteric Symbolism in Mozart's Masonic Opera: An Interpretation of the Libretto and the Music*. Rochester, VT: Inner Traditions International, 1992.

Chion, Michel. *The Voice in Cinema*. Trans. Claudia Gorbman. New York, NY: Columbia University Press, 1999.

Clément, Catherine. *Opera, or the Undoing of Women*. Trans. Betsy Wing. Minneapolis, MN: University of Minnesota Press, [1979] 1988.

Connor, Steven. *Dumbstruck: A Cultural History of Ventriloquism*. Oxford, UK: Oxford University Press, 2000.

Crenshaw, Kimberlee. 'Mapping the Margins: Intersectionality, Identity Politics and Violence Against Women of Color.' *Stanford Law Review* 43.6 (1991): 1241–1299.

Curtin, Adrian. *Avant-Garde Theatre Sound: Staging Sonic Modernity*. London, UK: Palgrave, 2014.

de Saussure, Ferdinand. *Course in General Linguistics*. Trans. Wade Baskin. New York, NY: Philosophical Library, 1959.

de Vries, Hilary. 'A Young Actress Extends Her Reach to the Stars'. *The New York Times*, 31 Dec. 1989. Sept. 2016 www.nytimes.com/1989/12/31/arts/theater-a-young-actress-extends-her-reach-to-the-stars.html?pagewanted=all [accessed 19 March 2017].

Derrida, Jacques. *Voice and Phenomenon*. Trans. Leonard Lawlor. Evanston, IL: Northwestern University Press, [1967] 2011.

Dinero, Dan. 'A Big Black Lady Stops the Show: Black Women, Performances of Excess and the Power of Saying No'. *Studies in Musical Theatre* 6.1 (2012): 29–41.

Dolar, Mladen. 'Preface: Is There a Voice in the Text?' *Sound Effects: The Object Voice in Fiction*. Eds. Jorge Sacido-Romero and Sylvia Mieszkowski. Leiden and Boston, MA: Brill Rodopi, 2015. xi–xx.

Dolar, Mladen. *A Voice and Nothing More*. Cambridge, MA: MIT Press, 2006.

Dunn, Leslie. 'Ophelia's Songs in *Hamlet*: Music, Madness, and the Feminine'. *Embodied Voices: Representing Female Vocality in Western Culture*. Eds. Leslie Dunn and Nancy A. Jones. New York, NY: Cambridge University Press, 1994. 50–64.

Dunn, Leslie, and Nancy A. Jones, eds. *Embodied Voices: Representing Female Vocality in Western Culture*. New York, NY: Cambridge University Press, 1994.

Edgerton, Michael Edward. *The 21st Century Voice: Contemporary and Traditional Extra-Normal Voice*. Baltimore, MD: Rowman & Littlefield Publishing, 2015.

Edison, Thomas. 'The Phonograph and Its Future'. *The North American Review* 126. 262 (1878): 527–536.

Eidsheim, Nina Sun. 'Sensing Voice: Materiality and the Lived Body in Singing and Listening'. *Voice Studies: Critical Approaches to Process, Performance and Experience*. Eds. Konstantinos Thomaidis and Ben Macpherson. London, UK and New York, NY: Routledge, 2015. 104–119.

Ex Machina. 'Lipsynch.' 2015. Sept. 2016 http://lacaserne.net/index2.php/theatre/lipsynch/ [accessed 19 March 2017].

Freyham, Michael. *The Authentic Magic Flute Libretto*. Toronto, ON and Plymouth, UK: The Scarecrow Press, 2009.

Fugate, Bradley K. *More than Men in Drag: Gender, Sexuality, and the Falsettist in Music Comedy of Western Civilization*. DMA dissertation. University of North Carolina at Greensboro, 2006.

Gener, Randy, ed. 'Approaches to Theatre Training: Pillars of Voice Work'. *American Theatre* 27.1 (2010).

Gillan, Matthew. 'Constructing the Okinawan Voice: Vocal Style, Aesthetics, and the Body in Okinawan Music'. *Journal of Interdisciplinary Voice Studies* 2.2 (2017) [forthcoming].

Ginther, Mihyang Amy. 'Dysconscious Racism in Mainstream British Voice Pedagogy and Its Potential Effects on Students from Pluralistic Backgrounds in UK Drama Conservatoires'. *Voice and Speech Review* 9.1 (2015): 41–60.

Hirschkind, Charles. *The Ethical Soundscape: Cassette Sermons and Islamic Counterpublics*. New York, NY: Columbia University Press, 2006.

Home-Cook, George. *Theatre and Aural Attention*. Basingstoke, UK: Palgrave Macmillan, 2015.

Inchley, Maggie. *Voice and New Writing, 1997–2007: Articulating the Demos*. London, UK: Palgrave Macmillan, 2015.

Jordanova, Ludmila. 'Natural Facts: A Historical Perspective on Science and Sexuality'. *Nature, Culture and Gender*. Eds. Carol P. MacCormack and Marilyn Strathern. Cambridge, UK: Cambridge University Press, 1980.

Kang, Heejae. 'An Acoustic and Laryngographic Study of Korean *Pansori* Singing'. MA thesis. University of London, 1999.

Kayes, Gillyanne. *Singing and the Actor*. London, UK: A & C Black Publishers, 2004.

Kimbrough, Andrew. *Dramatic Theories of the Voice in the Twentieth Century*. Amherst, NY: Cambria Press, 2011.

Knowles, Richard Paul. 'Shakespeare, Voice, and Ideology: Interrogating the Natural Voice'. *Shakespeare, Theory, and Performance*. Ed. James C. Bulman. London, UK: Routledge, 1996. 92–113.

Koestenbaum, Wayne. *The Queen's Throat: Opera, Homosexuality, and the Mystery of Desire*. New York, NY: Poseidon Press, 1993.

Kreiman, Jody & Diana Sidtis. *Foundations of Voice Studies: An Interdisciplinary Approach to Voice Production and Perception*. Malden, MA and Oxford, UK: Wiley-Blackwell, 2013.

Kristeva, Julia. *Revolution in Poetic Language*. Trans. Margaret Waller. New York, NY: Columbia University Press, [1974] 1984.

Kristeva, Julia. *Desire in Language: A Semiotic Approach to Literature and Art*. Ed. Leon S. Roudiez. New York, NY: Columbia University Press, 1980.

Linklater, Kristin. *Freeing the Natural Voice*. 2nd ed. London, UK: Nick Hern Books, [1976] 2006.

MacDonald, Claire, ed. *Performance Research: Voices* (Special Issue), 2003.

Martin, Jaqueline. *Voice in Modern Theatre*. London, UK: Routledge, 1991.

McAllister-Viel, Tara. 'Training Actors' Voices: Towards an Intercultural/ Interdisciplinary Approach'. *Voice Studies: Critical Approaches to Process, Performance and Experience*. Eds. Konstantinos Thomaidis and Ben Macpherson. London, UK and New York, NY: Routledge, 2015. 49–63.

McAllister-Viel, Tara. 'Speaking with an International Voice?' *Contemporary Theatre Review* 17.1 (2007): 97–106.

Miller, Richard. *On the Art of Singing*. Oxford: Oxford University Press, 1996.

Miller, Richard. *Training Soprano Voices*. New York, NY: Oxford University Press, 2000.

Muir, Marie-Louise. 'Fiona Shaw.' *BBC: ArtsExtra*, 30 Apr. 2012. Sept. 2016 www.bbc.co.uk/blogs/artsextra/2012/04/fiona-shaw.shtml [accessed 19 March 2017].

Neumark, Norie, Ross Gibson & Theo van Leeuwen, eds. *Voice: Vocal Aesthetics in Digital Arts and Media*. Cambridge, MA and London, UK: MIT Press, 2010.

Ochoa Gautier, Ana María. *Aurality: Listening and Knowledge in Nineteenth-Century Colombia*. Durham, NC: Duke University Press, 2014.

Papazoglou, Eleni. 'Introductory Note: Electra Speechless'. *Schene 2* (2011): 62.

Park, Chan E. *Voices from the Straw Mat: Toward an Ethnography of Korean Story Singing*. Honolulu, HI: University of Hawaii Press, 2003.

Piepenburg, Eric. 'He's Taking the 'Hood to the 1700's [*sic*]'. *The New York Times*, 6 Jan. 2012. Sept. 2016 www.nytimes.com/2012/01/08/theater/lin-manuel-miranda-is-rapping-on-alexander-hamilton.html?_r=0 [accessed 19 March 2017].

Pihl, Marshall R. *The Korean Singer of Tales*. Cambridge, MA: Harvard University Press, 1994.

Poizat, Michel. *The Angel's Cry: Beyond the Pleasure Principle in Opera*. Trans. Arthur Denner. Ithaca, NY: Cornell University Press, 1992.

Poole, Adrian, Deborah Warner & Fiona Shaw. '*Electra:* Practice and Performance I'. *Didaskalia* 5.3 (2002). Sept. 2016 www.didaskalia.net/issues/vol5no3/trans01.html [accessed 19 March 2017].

Potter, John. *Vocal Authority: Singing Style and Ideology*. Cambridge, UK: Cambridge University Press, 1998.

Potter, John & Neil Sorrell. *A History of Singing*. Cambridge, UK: Cambridge University Press, 2012.

Rebstock, Matthias & David Roesner, eds. *Composed Theatre: Aesthetics, Practices & Processes*. Bristol, CT: Intellect, 2012.

Reynolds, Bryan, ed. *Performance Studies: Key Words, Concepts and Theories*. London, UK: Palgrave Macmillan, 2014.

Richards, Mary. *Marina Abramovic*. London, UK and New York, NY: Routledge, 2010.

Ritsos, Yannis. *The Fourth Dimension*. Trans. Peter Green and Beverly Bardsley. Princeton, NJ: Princeton University Press, 1993.

Rodenburg, Patsy. *The Actor Speaks: Voice and the Performer*. Basingstoke, UK: Palgrave Macmillan, 2000.

Schafer, R. Murray. *The Soundscape: Our Sonic Environment and the Tuning of the World*. New York, NY: Knopf, 1977.

Schechner, Richard. *Performance Studies: An Introduction*. New York, NY: Routledge, [2001] 2013.

Schlichter, Annette. 'Un/Voicing the Self: Vocal Pedagogy and the Discourse-Practices of Subjectivation'. *Postmodern Culture* 24.3 (2014). Sept. 2016 www.muse.jhu.edu/article/589571 [accessed 19 March 2017].

Shaw, Fiona. 'Electra Speechless'. *Sophocles' Electra in Performance*. Ed. Francis M. Dunn. Stuttgart: M & P Verlag für Wissenschaft und Forschung, 1996. 131–138.

Shuttleworth, Ian. 'Electra'. *City Limits*, 1991. Sept. 2016 www.cix. co.uk/~shutters/reviews/91140.htm [accessed 19 March 2017].

Spencer, Charles. 'Random: Small Play, Big Punch.' 12 Mar. 2008. Sept. 2016 www.telegraph.co.uk/culture/theatre/drama/3671775/Random-Small-play-big-punch.html [accessed 19 March 2017].

Staniewski, Włodzimierz & Alison Hodge. *Hidden Territories: The Theatre of Gardzienice*. London, UK and New York, NY: Routledge, 2004.

Stark, James. *Bel Canto: A History of Vocal Pedagogy*. Toronto, ON: University of Toronto Press, 1999.

Stockburger, Axel. 'The Play of the Voice: The Role of the Voice in Contemporary Video and Computer Games'. *Voice: Vocal Aesthetics in Digital Arts and Media*. Eds. Norie Neumark, Ross Gibson & Theo van Leeuwen. Cambridge, MA and London, UK: MIT Press, 2010. 281–299.

Stoever, Jennifer Lynn. 'Fine-Tuning the Sonic Color-Line: Radio and the Acousmatic Du Bois'. *Modernist Cultures* 10.1 (2015): 99–118.

Taylor, Millie, ed. *Studies in Musical Theatre: If I Sing* (Special Issue). 2012.

Thomaidis, Konstantinos. 'The Vocal Body'. *Body and Performance*. Ed. Sandra Reeve. Devon, UK: Triarchy Press, 2013. 85–98.

Thomaidis, Konstantinos & Sarah Butcher. '"The Voice is the Guide to the Experience as Well as the Experience Itself": An Interview with non zero one'. *Journal of Interdisciplinary Voice Studies* 1.1 (2016): 71–84.

Thomaidis, Konstantinos & Ben Macpherson, eds. *Voice Studies: Critical Approaches to Process, Performance and Experience*. London, UK and New York, NY: Routledge, 2015.

Verstraete, Pieter. 'Cathy Berberian's *Stripsody* – An Excess of Vocal Personas in Score and Performance'. *Cathy Berberian: Pioneer of Contemporary Vocality*. Eds. Pamela Karantonis, Francesca Placanica, Anne Sivuoja-Kauppala & Pieter Verstraete. Farnham, UK: Ashgate, 2014. 67–85.

Werner, Sarah. 'Performing Shakespeare: Voice Training and the Feminist Actor'. *New Theatre Quarterly* 12.47 (1996): 249–258.

Whitman-Linsen, Candace. *Through the Dubbing Glass*. Frankfurt am Main: Peter Lang, 1992.

Wolf, Stacy. *Changed for Good: A Feminist History of the Broadway Musical*. New York, NY and Oxford, UK: Oxford University Press, 2001.

Young, Harvey. *Theatre & Race*. Basingstoke, UK: Palgrave Macmillan, 2013.

Young, Miriama. *Singing the Body Electric: The Human Voice and Sound Technology*. Farnham, UK: Ashgate, 2015.

index

2001: A Space Odyssey, 63

Abbate, Carolyn, 12, 36–8, 40, 46,
    47, 51, 72
Abramović, Marina, 57, 74
accent, 3, 22, 49, 50, 59, 63
acousmêtre, 62–4, 66, 67
activist voices and sound, 27, 70,
    71, 74
Adorno, Theodor W., 12, 61–2
anchor function, 5
Anderson, Laurie, 67
animality, 19, 20, 21, 31, 37
answering machine, 67
Aperghis, Georges, 27
archi-writing, 24
aria, 30, 32, 33, 34, 37, 38
Aristotle, 11, 16, 19–23, 36, 72
Artaud, Antonin, 27–9
ATHE, 10
aural body, 73
aurality, 59, 76

Austin, J.L., 9
authenticity effect, 68–9

Bakhtin, Mikhail, 54
Barba, Eugenio, 9, 29
Barthes, Roland, 45–6, 72
Beckett, Samuel, 29–30, 34
belting, 8, 40
Berberian, Cathy, 26
Berry, Cicely, 52, 57
Besson, Benno, 34
binaural recording, 69
Blythe, Alecky, 49
Bral, Grzegorz, 54
Brook, Peter, 29
Brown, Ross, 73
burlesque, 31
Butcher, Sarah, 3–4
Butler, Judith, 70

Cartwright, Jim, 62
cassette sermons, 69

Cavarero, Adriana, 12, 23–5, 51, 72
Chicago, 41
Chion, Michel, 12, 62–3, 72
choir, 25, 27
Chorus, 69–70
chorus, 21, 33, 72
class, 47, 49–50, 56
Clément, Catherine, 35–6, 40, 46, 51
coloratura, 34
communication, 5, 17, 20, 23–5, 29, 41, 46
composed theatre, 31
composition, 4, 26, 27, 31, 37, 45, 54
Connor, Steven, 12, 59–60, 72
Cork, Adam, 49
cry, 15, 35, 40, 43, 44

de Saussure, Ferdinand, 17
de-acousmatization, 63–4, 66
DeLaurenti, Christopher, 70, 74
Derrida, Jacques, 12, 23–5
Dessay, Natalie, 34
diction, 16
Dolar, Mladen, 12, 29, 31, 44
dubbing, 58, 74
Dunn, Leslie C., 39–40
dysconscious racism, 51

Edgerton, Michael Edward, 27
Edison, Thomas, 61
Eidsheim, Nina, 25
El Khoury, Tania, 71
Electra, 13–22, 26, 30, 73
envoicing, 38, 47
extra-normal voice, 27

falsetto, 42, 64
    falsettist, 41–2, 47
film, 58, 61–3, 67
Five Fathoms Opera Project, 25
Freeing the Voice, 57
Fret, Jarosław, 54
Fugate, Bradley, 41

Galás, Diamanda, 27
Gardens Speak, 71–2
Gardzienice, 54, 57
gay, 43, 44
gender, 12, 35, 38, 41–3, 46, 47, 56, 60
Götz, Cornelia, 33
Gough, Orlando, 27
grain of the voice, 45–6, 72
gramophone, 61–2
Grotowski, Jerzy, 29, 54

Hairspray, 47
Hamilton, 48
Hamlet, 39
Hart, Roy, 29
headphones, 2–4, 65, 68
hearing, 4, 24, 58
Herbert, Matthew, 69–70
Hirschkind, Charles, 69
Hofer, Josepha, 32
Home-Cook, George, 65

ideality, 18, 20, 25
ideology, 6, 37
IFTR, 10
immersion, 5, 11, 71
impersonator, 62
in-between
    voice as, 73–4

Infanti, Andrew, 25
installation, 11, 57, 69, 70, 71
interdisciplinarity, 11, 26
intersectionality, 41, 47–50, 56, 72
Istria, Évelyne, 15

Jones, Nancy A., 39–40

Kaegi, Stefan, 2, 4
Koestenbaum, Wayne, 43–5, 72
Kristeva, Julia, 46

La Barbara, Joan, 27
LaBelle, Brandon, 27
Lacan, Jacques, 44
lament, 27, 39
language, ix, 2, 17–31, 41, 45–7,
    71, 73
Lepage, Robert, 57
lexis, 16, 19
LGBTQ, 42
libretto, 31, 37
lieder, 45
linguistics, 11, 17
    linguistic aspects of communica-
        tion, 5, 18, 21, 24, 29, 30, 49
    non-linguistic sounds, 46
    postlinguistic phenomena, 31, 38
    prelinguistic phenomena, 31, 57
Linklater, Kristin, 52, 57
Lipsynch, 57–9, 63, 74
listening, xii, xiii, 1, 3, 6, 9, 11, 13,
    20, 24, 26, 31, 38–41, 43–5,
    47, 48, 51, 55, 56, 57, 58, 60,
    61, 62, 64, 68, 69, 70, 71
    plural listening, 72–3
    pod listening, 68

logos, 19, 21, 25, 31
    logocentrism, 23, 26, 29, 37
London Road, 49
Louise Attaque, 2
lyrics, 10, 26, 36, 47

Marshall, Nadine, 50
materiality
    of the voice, 17, 21, 23–30, 38,
        45, 47, 70
McBurney, Simon, 33
meaning, 16–20, 29–30, 38, 41, 44
megamusical, 39
melody, 16, 31
Menzel, Idina, 40
microphone, 64
Minton, Phil, 27
Miranda, Lin-Manuel, 48–9
Monk, Meredith, 27
Mozart, Wolfgang Amadeus, 31–2
music, 1, 4, 26–7, 29, 30–49, 56,
    67, 70, 71, 74
musical theatre, 8, 10, 11, 31,
    39–41, 44, 47–9, 71
musicology, 11, 37
mute, 30, 43

natural voice, 52–7
Neath, Glen, 68
Neumark, Norie, xi–xiii, 67
noise, 26, 29, 30
non zero one, 3

O Superman, 67
O'Haughey, Michael, 42
Ochoa Gautier, Ana María, 73
Okinawan music, 56

opera, 11, 25–6, 30–8, 41, 43–4,
    47, 51, 68, 73
Orestes, 15

pansori, 55–6, 57
Parret, Herman, 31
performative acts, 9
phone, 19, 21
phoneme, 12–20
phonograph, 59, 61
phonology, 19
Piesn Kozla, 54
pitch, 14, 18, 22, 31, 64, 66
pleasure, 13, 19, 27, 40, 44–5, 72
Poetics, 16–18, 23, 36
Poizat, Michel, 44–5, 72
Politics, 19–20
polyphony, 31, 54, 65, 71
pop, 39, 40
Potter, John, 12, 37
protests, 2, 70
psychoanalysis, 11, 44
psychology, 15, 46, 52, 53

Queen of the Night, 32–8, 40, 44
queer, 40, 43

race, 12, 47–8, 50, 56, 60
radio, 27, 28, 59, 63, 64
Random, 50
Received Pronunciation, 51
regionality, 11, 49, 56
registers, 34–5, 40–1, 42
Remote Paris, 1–7, 11, 65–7
Reynolds, Bryan, 9
Rimini Protokoll, 1, 65; *see also*
    Remote Paris

Ritsos, Yannis, 15
rock, 2, 40
Rodenburg, Patsy, 52, 57
Rosenberg, David, 68
Roussel, Gaëtan, 2

Schafer, R. Murray, 4
Schechner, Richard, 9
scream, 17, 18, 21, 27, 28, 29,
    30, 57
semiotics, 22, 45, 46
Shaw, Fiona, 14, 15, 18, 22, 30, 73
signification, 17, 20, 24, 72
    non-signifying voice and sound,
        30, 37, 44, 72
    presignifying voices, 31
    signifier, 17
silence, 1, 22, 29
    silencing, 21, 50
singing, 11, 25, 27, 30–40, 43, 45,
    54, 55, 68, 71
Snapper, Juliana, 25–6
song, 2, 16, 26, 27, 32, 35, 36, 39,
    40, 41, 43, 45, 47, 49, 54, 55,
    67, 73
    'big black lady' song, 47
    geno-song, 45
    pheno-song, 45
sonic color-line, 48
sonority, 23–30, 46, 71
Sophocles, 13
sound, xii, 2, 4, 6, 7, 11, 12, 18,
    19, 20, 21, 22, 25, 26, 27, 29,
    31, 34, 35, 41, 42, 43, 44, 45,
    46, 47, 48, 49, 50, 55, 56, 58,
    64, 65, 67, 68, 69, 70, 71, 73
    activist sound, 70

sound (*Continued*)
   non-verbal sound, 18, 27, 40
   sound designer, 11, 73
   sound signal, 4
   soundscape, 4, 72
   soundtrack, 4
speech, 10, 13–30, 37, 40, 44, 49,
     50, 58, 63, 72
   speech synthesis, 67
   speech training, 11, 52–3
   text-to-speech technology, 7
Staniewski, Włodzimierz, 54
Stockburger, Axel, 5
Stoever, Jennifer, 48, 72
Stripsody, 26
Štromajer, Igor, 68
synthesized voice, 7, 65, 67

TaPRA, 10
Teatr ZAR, 54
telephone, 7, 59, 64
text, xii, 2, 3, 4–5, 7, 8, 10, 11,
     13–18, 22, 24–8, 31, 33,
     36–8, 40, 43, 44, 47, 49, 51,
     53, 67, 71, 72, 73, 74
The Color Purple, 47
The Magic Flute, 31–3, 36
The Ring, 68–9

The Rise and Fall of Little Voice, 62
*To Have Done with the Judgement of
     God*, 28
To You, the Birdie!, 64
training, 29, 50–6, 73
transmission, 4, 17, 55, 59, 72
tucker green, debbie, 49

unsinging, 36
utterance, 1, 5, 9, 19–21, 29

Van Halen, 2
vaudeville, 31, 42
Vitez, Antoine, 15
vocalic body, 60–2, 66, 70, 71
vocality, 15–16, 20, 22, 31, 32, 39,
     57, 61
vocoder, 67
voice studies, 12
voice-over, 8, 58

Waiting for Godot, 29
Warner, Deborah, 13–15, 21, 30
Wicked, 39–40, 43
Wolf, Stacy, 40, 43
Wolfsohn, Alfred, 29
Wooster Group, 64

Young, Miriama, 68

acknowledgements

Warm thanks to Stefan Kaegi (Rimini Protokoll) and Ex Machina – for sharing documentation; to Adrian Curtin and Natalia Theodoridou – for taking the time to listen; to Amanda and Ben – for years of voicing; and to the series editors and the team at Palgrave – for their patient support.